You have a lot to offer.

We're asking you to volunteer.

Oakland-Alameda Endodontics
2930 Summit St.
Oakland, CA 94609
510-839-9480

Giving from Your Heart

Giving from Your Heart

✦

A Guide to Volunteering

Dr. Bob Rosenberg and Guy Lampard
Foreword by Robert K. Goodwin,
CEO Points of Light Foundation

iUniverse, Inc.
New York Lincoln Shanghai

Giving from Your Heart
A Guide to Volunteering

iUniverse books may be ordered through booksellers or by contacting:

iUniverse
2021 Pine Lake Road, Suite 100
Lincoln, NE 68512
www.iuniverse.com
1-800-Authors (1-800-288-4677)

ISBN: 0-595-34024-5

Printed in the United States of America

Contents

Acknowledgements

We have relied on the wisdom and experience of many people who were generous with their time and insights. In addition to the numerous people mentioned in this book, we would like to thank the following:

Suzanne Badenhoop; Tina Baylis; Mark Bergstrom; Al Bridwell; Meaghan Campion, Business Strengthening America; Allison Carl; Chuck Currie, Goose Hollow Family Shelter; Deborah M. Dalfen, Civic Ventures; Rick Danzansky; Cassandra Flipper, Bread and Roses; Jessica Gerock, Schoolhouse Supplies; Charlotte Coker Gibson, Points of Light Foundation; Paul Ginsburg; David Guggenhime; Skip Henderson, Fund Raising Counsel; Roccie Hill, Earthshare; Andrea Hurst; Rich Jenne, Cal Trout; Ed Kim, SF Habitat for Humanity; Mark Lasoff, Walk-In Counseling Center; Roger Macauley; Malcolm Margolin, Heyday Books; Peter Mazonas; Amanda Mortimer; Andy Nelson, Hands-On-Portland; Doreen Pollock, Make A Difference; Suzie Pollock, Center for Volunteer and Nonprofit Leadership of Marin; Alison J. Rapping, Make A Difference; Claude Rosenberg, New Tithing; Jerrold Rosenberg; Lisa Schlang, Center for Volunteer and Nonprofit Leadership of Marin; Tiffany Seifert; Dr.Tom Singer; Bob Wilkins; Jason Willett, VolunteerMatch; Ron Williams, Recovery Association Project; Jonathan Wilson, Center for Volunteer and Nonprofit Leadership of Marin.

Foreword

Unfortunately, we live in a disconnected society, a social structure that divides those who have the necessary abilities and resources to succeed from those who do not.

Sadly, many of us direct ourselves through life's steady stream of human traffic as safely as we can, taking few risks and avoiding the rich diversity society has to offer. For the most part, we walk in the mainstream with the comfort of knowing that others like us are walking in the same direction.

We're well aware of human beings who live beyond our own comfortable surroundings, but the images of them are fleeting, and we acknowledge them only intellectually. They eventually become nothing more than social mythology.

We are creatures of habit who become increasingly numb as familiar patterns within our lives repeat over and over again. We wake up, get dressed, eat breakfast, read the newspaper, go to the office, work in a job, attend a meeting, collect a paycheck, go home, socialize with friends, read a book, attend to personal business, go to bed, and sleep safely.

With time, the division between the fortunate and less fortunate grows, and we become increasingly disconnected from members of our own human family. Those who live or work beyond our familiar social environment are in danger of becoming more *invisible* as they are pushed to the very edge of our awareness.

It seems as though the less we look beyond our own comfort zones, the more we grow apart. The more we grow apart, the more invisible these people and their lives become to us. And then we stop caring. Unfortunately, the less we care, the more headlines we read about people who have been disconnected from society and pushed to their limits. In some cases, these are the people who express their anger and frustration through violence or depression.

In the end, preventing and solving serious social problems comes down to addressing very basic human needs: people are struggling to survive and are doing so alone. They are not connected to the necessary community resources, relationships, or human assistance they require to reach their full potential in our society.

Fortunately, in *Giving from Your Heart*, Bob Rosenberg and Guy Lampard provide us with unique insight and inspiration about the value of sharing through volunteering. Their compelling stories are evidence that while we are certainly a nation of communities, we are foremost a community of people. That's why it's so important to continually look for opportunities to help people reconnect to each other, to their communities, and to the necessary resources within their communities. *Giving from Your Heart* is proof positive that people are the solution.

Bob Rosenberg and Guy Lampard's inspirational stories and logical approach to effective volunteering will help to illuminate a path toward satisfying and effective experiences. Ultimately, "we, the people" are the ones who make the choices about our future. If we hold the solution to society's serious problems, then our responsibilities must be to each other. If we're successful in building a better society for the future, perhaps today's serious social problems will be remembered simply as the growing pains of our past.

In the end, the spirit of volunteering may be the only way to change the world.

Robert K. Goodwin
President & CEO, Points of Light Foundation

Introduction

We are at our best when we share with others. Whether it is knowledge, money, or simply time, people gain when they give. This book is about sharing yourself through volunteering.

Many of us already volunteer and are reaping the personal rewards from doing so. If you have not yet become involved, the chances are good that you've given it some thought but see obstacles, real or imaginary, that prevent you from taking the step that will connect you with a volunteer opportunity. We wrote *Giving from Your Heart: A Guide to Volunteering* because we want you to take action, to share in the mutual rewards, for you and your community, of volunteering. During the past few years we have heard and read about volunteers who have served their communities in a variety of ways. However, until now there has not been a resource for the individual who wants to know where to go and whom to ask about which community service activity is right for them. This book provides such information for anyone considering volunteering in a down-to-earth manner.

Researching this book took us to different cities across the country and introduced us to a wide variety of people, all connected by the same thread, a commitment to volunteering. Dozens of volunteers, executive directors, board of directors members, and salaried staff provided much of the inspiration and solid recommendations that follow. We hope that you will be inspired, as we have been, by those whose stories we tell.

Like many of our peers approaching or realizing retirement, we are anticipating many more years of productivity. Now we are looking forward to rewarding community service work that will be quite different from our former occupations, Bob as an endodontist (root canal specialist) and Guy as an investment banking marketing specialist. We feel that in many ways our best years lie ahead. We are excited about further exercising our passion to involve ourselves and others in the possibilities presented by volunteering.

We hope you are too.

This book is for everyone, from teens to seniors, singles and families. Yet we do focus on those who are either retired or approaching retirement, people with more time to give. That's because in addition to living longer, people are living more active lives well into their senior years. Baby boomers comprise over 77 million individuals, or a whopping 29 percent of our population, and are on the brink of major changes in how they spend their time. Through volunteering, they can help to solve the social and environmental issues that our nation is facing. Volunteerism cannot solve all our problems, but it has the potential to have a major impact on communities, on recipients, and on the volunteers themselves.

We have written this for your enlightenment and your enjoyment. As authors, we have several goals. We will educate you about the world of nonprofit organizations, the route to many volunteer opportunities. We will provide you with the tools to decide what type of volunteer you want to be, to choose what type of activity you want to do, and to make the connection with the volunteer opportunity that's right for you. But most importantly, we want to inspire you to volunteer. It may be the most positive experience of your life.

Kathleen Murray

In January of 2002, Kathleen Murray began a remarkable journey, hopscotching across the country to volunteer for a month at a time at over a dozen organizations in as many states. Her goal was to work for causes she cared deeply about, such as children's issues, poverty, and aging. At the same time, this work provided her a podium from which to raise awareness of the importance for more volunteerism nationally. Her stops included an assisted-living center in New Orleans, a homeless organization for youth in San Diego, and a neo-natal clinic in Atlanta. Kathleen believes that much of the inspiration for her involvement in charitable causes stems from her caring family and the kindness she witnessed while growing up.

"I am fortunate to have so much abundance in my life. My aunt and my mother did not make me feel that it was my duty or obligation to give back but rather my privilege and my honor to be able to share and pass along some of the blessings I was able to receive."

Kathleen provided some practical advice for those new to volunteering. "Firstly, what really is most important is the act of getting involved. People are transformed by showing up to help others. It matters less how much time one can give than the fact that there is a commitment made. Without any hesitation or doubt in my mind, I can say that kindness is contagious. Before making a major commitment of your time to a nonprofit organization, do your research. You do the research when you buy a car. Here, you're putting your time out there, and that's at least as important as a car. Treat it like a job interview. If you don't get what you're expecting, you could end up unhappy and just not show up. And that might taint your entire experience. If in the course of the interview the experience doesn't feel right, keep looking until you find the right opportunity. Also, many volunteer tasks require training, and organizations should be equipped to provide the training necessary. If you are going to work in a hospice, you need to know the laws concerning hospice care, and you need training in counseling as well."

Kathleen is someone who has touched the lives of many, and her commitment inspires others. To hear her talk, though, you realize that it is she who feels blessed. Like many that we have met, Kathleen feels that helping others gives one so much in return.

"I have fallen in love with my life. To be able to live with purpose is a gift that far exceeds any expectation I might ever have had. My only hope is that I will be able to give back just a tenth of what I have received. To live life filled with passion is the personification of success and reminds me of my favorite quote from Margaret Mead:

'Never doubt that a small group of thoughtful, committed people can change the world; indeed, it's the only thing that ever has!'"

1

Getting Started

Harry Anixter stands at the front of a cramped makeshift classroom. He faces a group of nine intently interested students. They watch as Harry turns and scrawls a sentence on the blackboard. The adult students pick up their pencils and begin to translate the Spanish phrase into English. One woman is nursing her infant daughter as she writes on the paper. Harry patiently waits as they wrestle with the words.

Harry is retired. For the past five years he has filled his free time and satisfied his desire to give by volunteering as an English teacher at the Good Samaritan Family Resource Center in San Francisco. His students are mostly Latino and Asian.

For Harry, like many, the prospect of retiring was scary. When he turned sixty-five, he decided the best way to prepare for his free time was to plan for it.

"A lot of my friends don't retire because they don't know what they would do if they did," he says. So the year before he stopped working, Harry went to school to study Spanish. He was referred to the Good Samaritan Center, where he was interviewed by Anne Marie Sullivan, who ran the educational program. "Since the salary was not a question—there is none—she hired me right away."

His three-day-per-week commitment quickly evolved to four, and on his off day he volunteers for the Humane Society. He loves what he does. "It has to suit your fancy—there are a lot of volunteer things I would not do. There is a tremendous gratification in seeing people learn. After being in the business world and doing things at times that you did not like, when you retire, you want to do something that you do like."

Harry is like most of us in his desire to give to others, but initially he did not know where to turn or how to get connected. But Harry pursued his passion, made the connection and is now making a difference in the lives of those he touches. Whether we are retired, about to retire, or decades away, we want to make our lives meaningful, and volunteering can help us realize this goal.

Harry Anixter and Anne Marie Sullivan with a student at the Good Samaritan House in San Francisco

If someone were to approach you about volunteering, and he or she told you that you could choose your level of commitment and work in an area of volunteerism that was close to your heart, you would probably answer, "When do I start?" The following are a few basic questions to help you on your way.

Think for a minute about what grabs you, what you care about more than anything besides your family and your faith. For what do you have a passion? What makes your jaws tighten when you hear about it, makes you wish that you had a chance to make a difference? Children, the developmentally disabled, stray kittens, oil spills, a family member with diabetes. What really goes to your core? We will not prioritize your concerns—that is up to you. Write a couple of your thoughts below and dog-ear the page. We'll be coming back here.

_____

_____

HOW MUCH?

Before volunteering, one of the first things you have to do is assess your level of involvement. You'll have to make the best use of your abilities and time in order to maximize your effectiveness. For those already involved, you may be ready and able to increase your involvement, perhaps from an episodic commitment to one that is more consistent or long term.

As you consider your volunteer commitment, you should be thinking about the "how much" questions. How much time? How much money, if any? How much of me?

The answers to all three will probably change over time. The amount of time available to you now may be much less than after you retire or after your children leave for college. For many, as available time increases, so does their level of involvement. Your level of financial support may be minimal or nonexistent when you become involved in the organization. Unless you are on the board of directors, you may not find yourself contributing at all. We'll talk more about this in Chapter 3. However, as you become more engaged in the nonprofit organization, it is likely that your level of financial support will increase. Finally, How much of me? How much will I give of my heart and soul? The answer lies within you. If you are able to exercise your passion, your life may be changed by the volunteer experience. The question may be rephrased, How much am I willing to be transformed by the giving of my time and energies?

LEVELS OF INVOLVEMENT

Driving the elderly to their medical appointments once a month requires a different kind of commitment than becoming an internationally based healthcare volunteer for a year. Both are needed, yet each demands a different level of research and training. For the purposes of creating guidelines, we have divided volunteer involvement into three broad categories: one-time or intermittent volunteering, ongoing volunteering, and "mega-commitment."

One-time or Intermittent Volunteering

Many nonprofits are in desperate need of volunteers for activities that do not require a huge commitment of time, expertise, or training. Delivering meals to shut-ins, cleaning a stretch of beach, collecting clothing for those in need, and thousands of similar volunteer opportunities can be found every day of the year. Most ask only that you show up on time with a smile on your face and a willingness to help.

Ongoing Volunteering

There are other volunteer opportunities that require a longer term commitment. Children needing long-term assistance respond much better if they have continuity with volunteers. Mentoring programs are successful when children and mentors develop real and trusting relationships. This does not happen overnight, but over a period of time. Many volunteer positions involve training and utilize the nonprofit's staff and other resources in order to provide such training. Most nonprofits are operating on a shoestring and cannot afford to train volunteers who do not stick around.

Mega-Commitment

This is a sustained commitment requiring a significant amount of time and energy, for example, a year overseas in rural agricultural development. We spoke to a man in his late sixties who had retired and then fulfilled a lifelong dream of becoming a Peace Corps volunteer. He was in the U.S. for a brief time before returning to Romania to continue his volunteer assignment. Many countries, including our own, are deeply appreciative of volunteers who make extended commitments in faraway places. Whether in rural Vermont or Nairobi, people who bring skills to areas in need are transformed by the process as well as transforming those who receive such assistance.

After interviewing volunteers, nonprofit executive directors, presidents of boards of directors, and consultants to the nonprofit community, we have come up with some tips on making your best decision for volunteering. We have taken what we think are the best recommendations, as well as a few of our own, and incorporated them into the following guidelines. Some great advice can also be found at www.networkforgood.org and at www.serviceleader.org. Listed below are universal guidelines. Additional guidelines for long-term commitment are presented in Chapter 6.

How Can I Serve Best?

1. Exercise your passion

Volunteer for an organization with which you identify, that shares your ideals and involves something you care about. Chances are there are many, and it may take a bit of research to find the best fit. Are you passionate about the environment? Do something about it by involving yourself in one of the thousands of planet-saving organizations. Are you interested in children? In literacy? In helping the disabled? In providing assistance for the elderly? Volunteer opportunities abound in whatever arena you have an interest. It is likely that you will enjoy your volunteer work more and be a more effective volunteer if you involve yourself with something you are passionate about.

2. Be realistic about your time commitment

If you are a full-time working mom with two kids at home, chances are you have less available time than a retired teacher. You may be passionate about teaching kids to read, but you may only have an hour every so often. Now is not the time to over-commit but to realistically gauge your availability. Conversely, you may be a retiree who loves to play golf. Since it doesn't take all day, every day to enjoy the game, you probably have ample time to make a longer-term commitment.

3. Figure out what you bring to the table

We all have skills. Some tasks require a greater degree of formal and on-the-job training than others, but volunteer opportunities exist for each of us. If you have special education or training, you may put this knowledge to use as a volunteer and be valuable because of it. On the other hand, you may wish to involve yourself in something unrelated to your field of work or endeavor. Most of the time, your heart is the most valuable asset you will bring to the organization.

4. Decide what you can learn in the process

A substantial number of volunteer opportunities involve volunteer training. You may be able to develop new skills and knowledge while performing needed services. This should not be your primary motivator, but learning is always of value. Sharon Bernstein is on the staff of Hands On Portland (an affiliate of the Hands On Network—see Appendix A), an organization that provides episodic volunteer opportunities. She always asks, "After giving back, what is your second reason for volunteering?" There is nothing wrong with having motivations in addition to the simple desire to help. How great would you feel if you made a substantial contribution to people's lives, or to the environment, while learning new skills you could use for the rest of your life?

THE "HOW CAN I SERVE BEST" QUESTIONNAIRE

Ask yourself the following questions:

1. For what do I really have a passion? _____

2. How much time can I realistically commit at this point in my life?

    Hours per week _____
    Hours per month _____

3. After "giving back," what is my second reason for volunteering?

    a. _____ to meet people
    b. _____ to develop job skills
    c. _____ to occupy free time
    d. _____ to travel
    e. _____ to combine work skills with travel
    f. _____ to network
    g. _____ to build my resume
    h. _____ to do something rewarding with family/friends
    i. _____ to get to know the community better
    j. _____ to meet a potential spouse or someone to date
    k. _____ to obtain a school or job requirement
    l. _____ to learn how to do new things
    m. _____ to see if I like it
    n. _____ to achieve some other goal

4. What type of job do I want?

    a. _____ a hands-on task
    b. _____ service on the board of directors
    c. _____ virtual volunteering (volunteering from home)
    d. _____ an administrative position
    e. _____ one where I can use my own skills

5. If I commit to a long-term opportunity, will I be able to attend training sessions?

     Yes_____

     No_____

As we have mentioned, your commitment today will unlikely be your commitment tomorrow. Our lives and circumstances constantly change, hopefully for the better. As more time becomes available to us, many of us will move from episodic volunteering to longer-term commitments. As we do, we find ourselves in a more favorable position to lead with our hearts, to fully engage in something with which we have fallen in love.

Shawn Michael

If people volunteer as children, the chances increase that they will develop a life-long pattern of contributing. Shawn Michael is one of millions of young people who have followed this path. His high school in the Washington, D.C., suburbs ran a summer camp for five weeks, and a teacher asked him to give it a look, since the camp was looking for more male counselors. Considering that 80 percent of the counselors were female (and that they went to the pool every day), he decided to take a peek, so to speak. The campers were from low socio-economic areas and were matched one-to-one with counselors. The focus was on establishing relationships with kids who are primarily from single-parent homes. During the day, the counselor would stay with the kids during the activities. The program's goal was to place these children with people who would care about them and nurture them in a safe, comfortable environment.

Shawn did it for seven to eight summers, the last four years as a staff member.

"I did it the first summer and fell in love with it. The first summer, the kid was the toughest. It was therefore more rewarding. I became addicted. I felt selfish, because I came away with such a great feeling. You come away learning more from them than they did from you.

"I've rearranged my summers for camp. I'm teaching special education now, partially as a result of having summers off." By the way, he did get to meet girls that he would not otherwise have met.

"For me, this has been the ultimate humbling experience. Even if I have a pretty demanding career, I'll still find time to do something like this. I'm not going to win any awards, but there is still that satisfaction knowing that you've made a difference."

2

Volunteering by Age and Other Groupings

What is the best age to volunteer? Depending on your interests and time constraints, it could be now. In general, we volunteer more hours when we are older and have more time to give than when we are younger and find ourselves being pulled in a hundred different directions. It is not likely that a high school student will be able to devote the same number of hours as a retiree. You should *do what you can do when you can*. The U.S. Department of Labor reported the following volunteer statistics for the year September 2001 to September 2002.

Volunteers By Age Groupings

Age	Volunteered (%)	1–49 Hours (%)	100–499 Hours(%)	Median # Hours
16–19	26.9	53.1	22	40
20–24	18.2	53.1	22	36
25–34	25.1	55.7	23.2	34
35–44	34.4	45.8	27.8	52
45–54	31.4	43.5	29.7	53
55–64	27.5	50.4	32.2	60
65 and Over	22.7	33.4	35.4	96

While older adults who volunteer are devoting more hours than younger folks, a lower percentage of seniors are involved. One of our goals is to increase the number of people who volunteer, especially at older ages.

You've considered the level of commitment you are ready to make at this time in your life, and you've given some thought to the direction in which your heart is leading you. There are many volunteer possibilities based on age, family, and social groupings, some of which you may not have considered.

WHAT GROUP DO YOU FALL INTO?

Children (Under 12)

It is not likely that your seven-year-old is going to get involved in a volunteer situation on his or her own. At the same time, there is a wide variety of educational, religious, social, and service organizations than can accommodate involvement at a young age. For youngsters, most of what they will do at these young ages will be done with their families. The awareness developed is possibly more valuable than the tasks they perform. This will be discussed below.

Teens and Service Learning

If your teenage years were anything like ours, you are aware of the perils involved. Our goal is to help teenagers channel the vast amounts of hormonally generated energy they have in the proper direction. Take heart, for it can be done (to some extent). Perhaps the most exciting educational concept to emerge in recent years has been service learning.

While academicians long ago were including service to the community as part of the learning experience, it has only recently been codified and given national attention. According to the National and Community Service Trust Act of 1993:

Service learning is a method whereby students learn and develop through active participation in thoughtfully organized service that is conducted in and meets the needs of communities. It is coordinated with an elementary school, secondary school, institution of higher education, or community service program and the community.

Service learning helps foster civic responsibility.

Service learning is integrated into and enhances the academic curriculum of the students, or the education components of the community service program in which the participants are enrolled.

Service learning provides structured time for students or participants to reflect on the service experience.

Examples of service-learning projects include: preserving native plants, designing neighborhood playgrounds, teaching younger children to read, testing the local water quality, creating wheelchair ramps, preparing food for the homeless, developing urban community gardens, starting school recycling, and more.

The gamut of programs within a school is limited only by the imagination of the students, faculty, and community. A number of National Service Learning Leader Schools have been recognized for their creativity and commitment to this concept. We spoke to several program leaders, whose enthusiasm for the program was contagious.

The service-learning program at Tamarind Middle School of Warrington, PA, started in 1993. Tricia Eakins, long involved with the program, explained what it has meant to her students. "When the kids reach out to other people, it does a lot for their self-esteem. When service learning is tied to curriculum, they receive hands-on learning. It becomes more meaningful to them. The programs have made service a goal for these kids for the rest of their lives. It has become ingrained in their lives. It's become a way of life."

Greely High School is in the suburbs of Portland, Maine where Melissa Ska-han has been the director of its service-learning program for the past six years. "I see teens as full partners. The norm is for them to participate civically. A lot of people and an administrative team are empowered to make this happen. It's just the way we do business." They have all of the sophomores involved in the pro-gram, and each student will have had two to three service learning experiences prior to graduation. She sees a lot of benefits. "Once you have a positive service experience, it's hard not to go down that road again. It is so much a part of what we do. I'll just put out an announcement—it will run one day and we will get a large volume of students. It's what they do."

Ask your school administrators if service learning is part of the curriculum for your children. Whether in a formal school program or not, teens can be active volunteers. Camp counseling, assisting the elderly, and helping to clean nearby parks are a few ways teens can get involved. By integrating community service into the civic fabric, we can create generation after generation of men and women who see volunteerism as a way of life.

Twenty-Somethings, Thirty-Somethings, and Singles

The roughly two decades between our teenage years and the years in which we begin to show some gray are among the busiest of our lives. Finishing school, hopefully finding employment, getting married, and raising families manage to take up a fair amount of our time. It is likely that you will not have all of the time you want for volunteering. For many, finding the time is barely conceivable. For those who are able to volunteer, their efforts may be episodic. As we have mentioned, it is absolutely okay to *do what you are able to do, when you are able to do it.*

In hundreds of cities, volunteer clearinghouses provide listings of opportunities for those with limited time. One such group is Make A Difference, in Phoenix. Rick Hewton is a group leader for Saturday-morning kickball with developmentally disabled adults of the Civitan House. "This is more like playing than volunteering. I'm looking forward to it. It's an opportunity to build leadership skills." We asked why he does it. "Giving back to the community, meeting new friends, a good way to meet folks and have a social life outside work," he said. He has dated some of the women he has met through volunteering. "If you meet a woman doing volunteer work, you get the idea that she is a good person. You instantly have something in common." Though it does not advertise this fact, according to Rick, "Make A Difference is a premier dating service. Some of my best friends are people I've met volunteering. You meet people in a nonthreatening environment."

Saturday morning Kickball at the Civitan House in Phoenix

The Salvation Army housing project in Phoenix holds softball games for the kids who live there. Tom is one of the volunteers who make it happen. "I found out about this through a radio ad, and with my hectic schedule it works out real well." His advice: "It's easy. First of all, get out and do it. You can sit on the couch on a Saturday morning or go to a volunteer activity. I almost view it as self-ish, because the kids need it, but I love it. I'd love to volunteer full time if I could support myself."

His enthusiasm for volunteering was evident. "I don't drink and don't go to bars. People that volunteer are quality people. If I'm going to meet that special person, the likelihood is that it will be at a volunteer event."

In fact, there are volunteer organizations designed especially for singles. In 1997, Nikki Clifford heard about one such effort in Vermont and decided to start a similar organization in the Washington, D.C., area. Today, Singles Volunteers of D.C. (SVDC) has 8,800 members. SVDC, via its electronic newsletter, advertises between five and twenty activities per week to its members. Each activity has a team leader who coordinates an informal get-together before or after the volunteer activity. Care is taken to balance the number of men and women at each event.

Nikki first met her future husband at an SVDC event in 1999. They met again at another sponsored event while sorting sweet potatoes for a local soup kitchen. In 2002, they were married. Since 1997, there have been forty-five marriages because of SVDC! When asked why this sort of environment is better for meeting people, Nikki said, "It is much more relaxed and certainly doesn't have that 'meat market' feel the bar scene does. Also, you are surrounded by like-minded people with common values about helping others."

Couples of All Ages

For many couples, economics demand that both partners work. Just finding time to spend with each other is a challenge. Why not spend that time together volunteering?

One Thursday evening, Beverly and Bill were volunteering at the Schoolhouse Supplies warehouse in Portland, Oregon. "When we have the time, we just sign up." Their advice: "Just sign up and do it. It's not as hard as it seems." Hands On Portland has a calendar on its Web site that they use to check against their schedules. "Think about two to three weeks ahead and just show up. For some people it is awkward at first. But five or ten minutes go by and then you're into it."

Phil and Susan Midell are project leaders at the Salvation Army softball event in Phoenix. "We retired and wanted to do something together. It's good for our relationship."

Families

The time when we are at our most productive economically is usually our busiest, with career, family, the acquisition of material wealth, including houses, automobiles, and the things that fill them with clutter. We do those things for which we have been programmed, and the time passes so quickly that there may be little time for introspection. Even so, a lot of us volunteer and don't call it volunteering. We are active in the PTA, in our kids' athletic teams, in business and professional organizations, in our houses of worship, and in many other activities. Obviously coaching your kids brings you into a different form of contact than sitting in front of the TV and fighting for control of the remote. Yet much of what we do during these years does not involve family as much as we would like it to. Volunteer opportunities that the entire family can enjoy are a great way to instill the value of giving back to the community while having fun together. Family opportunities exist in nonprofits such as the One Brick organization of San Francisco, which needs help in inspecting and repackaging donated food for the hungry. Numerous habitat-renewal projects love to have families help in the process. The Little Brothers-Friends of the Elderly visits isolated elders, bringing them food, and it also welcomes family involvement.

The Transitional Center in Portland provides interim housing for men who are making changes in their lives and aiming for greater productivity. On a fall evening in Portland, Ashley, a local teenager, her mom, sister, and group of volunteers were preparing dinner for the residents. She has vivid memories of her sixth Christmas, when her mother took her around the neighborhood to distribute gifts to those in need. She feels good volunteering. She also knows that colleges look favorably on community service. Ashley's mom sees another benefit to volunteering. "We don't realize what we have until we do things like this."

Bob Michael is an old (or should we say aging) friend from high school who has been successful in his law career in suburban Washington, D.C. He and his wife, Anne, have made volunteering as a family a priority. "The best benefit is what we got as a family. We have given our kids everything, and they really don't know about others. This is a way to show them another side of the world. It has helped to create balance in my kids; they have a greater appreciation for what they have. When you pull away from the distractions of our normal lives, you pull together and grow closer as a family."

Ashley and family preparing dinner at the Transitional House, in Portland

Bill Lorton has been a consultant in the nonprofit community and is currently the executive director of the San Francisco's Habitat for Humanity. His feelings concerning volunteering with your family are as follows: "It is not as great for the organization in the short term, but it's a tremendous strategy in the long term." What Ashley's mom, Bob and Anne Michael, and Bill Lorton know is that they are building a life-long commitment within their children. It truly is a tremendous strategy.

OVER 40: PEOPLE WHO HAVE A LOT TO GIVE

Some of us aren't getting any younger. In fact a large number of us are growing older with varying degrees of gracefulness, a trend that will accelerate as baby boomers reach their sixties. Many are living the American Dream, enjoying a standard of living higher than that of our parents, possessing more advanced education, and foreseeing the day when the mortgage will be paid off.

Right now there are three distinct groups of those forty and older: baby boomers, active agers, and seniors. As time goes on, the distinctions will become blurred as life expectancy and geriatric health increases. It doesn't matter into which of these categories one falls; it is the collective volunteer participation of these groups that has the potential to dramatically enhance the nonprofit effort.

Baby Boomers

The year 1946 is considered the beginning of that period in our history known as the baby boom. Births increased from 2.85 million in 1945 to over 3.4 million in 1946, and things did not slow down until 1964. The boomer population swelled to 77 million over this period of eighteen years. That's a lot of folks who are going to have a lot of potentially productive time on their hands during the next several decades. For many boomers, now is a time of planning, formal or otherwise. Despite the setback in the stock markets during the past several years, a huge wave of soon-to-be-retired boomers is contemplating the future. Some will continue to work out of financial need; others will work because they actually like it. Many will work on a part-time basis for the same reasons. And large numbers will retire from the working world altogether. For those who will have more free time, a big question looms: What in the world am I gonna do now?

The past twenty-five to thirty-five years have been a time for raising families, getting out of bed to go to work, and accumulating piles of goods long since out of use. Many boomers have been involved in communities, schools, and places of worship. Some have traveled and pursued hobbies. Others have spent their lives on the job, whether at the office or behind the den door in the evening. Large numbers have not taken the time to do much else, and there is a lurking fear of the great unknown: *free time.*

Volunteer opportunities can provide the answer to the question of how to occupy those hours previously spent on the job. It is likely that many people will start out in short-term or episodic volunteer assignments. As more time becomes available, and as individuals narrow their areas of interest, a greater number will commit to long-term volunteer situations. This group will provide a large cadre of mentors, readers, and leaders in the nonprofit community.

Active Agers

This is the group of people that currently fall between the boomers and seniors. Sometime during the past half-century, the term "middle age" was redefined.

Despite the fact that one can't jump as high or run as fast, the terms "middle age," "elderly," "geriatric" are now seen as more of a mindset than anything physical. Marc Freedman, author of *Prime Time: How Baby Boomers Will Revolutionize Retirement and Transform America*, describes a new type of aging:

> There is a new style of life among people fifty-five to seventy, with a lot of people outside of each end that got stuck in between midlife and old age. The society is not exactly structured for that. This is not going to be the retirement of their parents. How can we create prototypes for people to think about the next chapter, forms of engagement that are going to be fulfilling?

We think that a good term for the people described by Marc is "active agers." And they aren't growing old quietly.

Many active agers, and certainly the boomers who follow, will be retired for many years. Some will actually be retired for more years than they worked. They are living longer, healthier, more active lives and are looking for personal satisfaction in new fields of endeavor. For them, volunteering is a way to stay active, to become involved, and to make those years meaningful and productive. As we have seen in many of the volunteer stories, productivity and a sense of self-worth does not necessarily have anything to do with earning money.

Many different reasons motivate active agers to get involved in long-term volunteer opportunities. Some volunteer because they always have, only now they can give it more time. Others volunteer because they fear looking across the kitchen table at their spouse of thirty-five years, having nothing to do and nowhere to go. Many are opting for volunteer work because they want to interact with others, to continue to exercise their minds, and, in some cases, to get out of the house for a while. Whatever the reasons, those who find their passion are no longer having trouble filling up the day with meaningful pursuits. The key has been finding and then exercising that passion.

Ruben Miller is the supervisor at a building site for Habitat for Humanity in San Francisco. He started as a vacation volunteer, working on a site in Central America. He donated $450 and paid his own way to get to the site. "I've always volunteered. When I retired, Habitat for Humanity asked me to become a construction manager. For me, it has given me a new perspective on life and what retirement means. I can't think of anything I'd rather be doing."

He adds, "People are becoming more aware of volunteer activity after retirement. I enjoy getting up in the morning and going to work. I can't think of myself sitting in front of the TV or golfing or fishing. This is like a second life. It is rewarding to be of service to people less fortunate than we are." For those intimidated about jumping in, "People say, 'I'm not sure I can do that.' There really is no need for that feeling."

Not everyone finds it so easy. Sometimes it takes time to find out what you want to do. Joel Kudler, a retired dentist, shared some hard-earned insight. He has volunteered as a hospital worker, injured bird feeder, truck driver for the Marine Mammal Center, instructor at the University of California in San Francisco School of Dentistry, and, perhaps the toughest of all, CASA (Court Appointed Special Advocate) caseworker, among a few other things. "When you wake up the next morning after you've retired, you realize that you can't go sailing or play golf all the time. A volunteer has to know oneself—what it is that makes you happy, what makes you tick. You should do things that make you happy. I really looked."

For Joel, the hard part was finding what ignited his passion. "I believe I can do anything, but I don't know what to do. Once you realize that you are responsible for your actions, you take responsibility for your life and make it happen. It is a very individual thing, volunteering." He summarized, "[Volunteering itself] is easy to do; what was hard for me was figuring out what to do."

Joel speaks for a lot of us when he honestly describes the trial and error of finding the cause that reaches inside us and goes to the core of our beings. The good news is that when you find it, you'll know it.

Seniors

People are so active these days that it is getting a bit tricky to define the term "senior citizen." An easy way would be to relate it strictly to age. Is seventy the number? How about seventy-two or seventy-five? Maybe you become a senior when you reach eighty. Perhaps becoming a senior has to do with one's health and self-sufficiency. For many, it is about attitude. You are a senior when you think and act like one, whatever that means. Regardless, there exist increasing numbers of volunteer activities in which our older citizens will make enormous contributions, both to each other and to society as a whole.

John W. Gardner, former secretary of the Department of Health, Education, and Welfare, was a founder of the Experience Corps and sat on the board of Civic Ventures. He shared his vision for senior citizens.

> We believe, without being immodest, that the large numbers of us over age sixty-five constitute a rich reservoir of talent, experience, and commitment potentially available to society. We believe that this will be a great adven-

ture—good for us physically and in every other way. If one lists the problems of older people, health would perhaps top the list, with economic problems perhaps second. After that, high on the list is a cluster of problems: loneliness, boredom, and the need to be needed. We believe that our plan hits directly at that cluster. And the current opinion in medical circles is that if one can deal with those problems, many of our problems of physical health will be more easily solved.

In fact, senior involvement is increasing, as reported in Peter D. Hart's report, *The New Faces of Retirement: An Ongoing Survey of American Attitudes on Aging.* The survey, based on phone interviews with people from fifty to seventy-five years old, showed a trend toward greater civic engagement, but one that falls short of involving all of those who have an interest. It appears that increasing numbers of seniors would become involved if the right kind of volunteer opportunities were available. While some are interested in modest financial compensation, that does not appear to be the primary factor in the decision to commit.

Practically speaking, one barrier to involvement is simply that people do not know where to go or whom to ask about volunteering. Seniors are much less likely to have Internet access or to be comfortable enough with computers to search for volunteer opportunities. The nonprofit community will have to seek out seniors where they live in order to maximize their participation.

Senior volunteers are active in the Foster Grandparent/Senior Companion programs. Program Director Kathy Smeland brings a group of them together for monthly lunches in Tiburon, California, where they share their experiences. They sit in a circle and talk about what they've been doing. They laugh easily and seem to enjoy the camaraderie. What they all agree on is the value of the volunteer experience in their lives. Douglas Tsou works with kindergarteners in arts, reading, writing, and math. He especially loves arriving at school. "Kids grab my arms, my legs—I love it. They love me more than my own grandkids. They make me happy."

BRING A FRIEND: THE MORE THE MERRIER

No matter what your age, there is a certain amount of anxiety that accompanies placing yourself in an uncomfortable or unfamiliar position. This fear of the unknown is what keeps many of us from offering to volunteer. Like many things in life, once you are involved, you wonder why you didn't do it sooner. But making that first step can seem like climbing a mountain. Why do it alone? Take along a friend, a relative, a co-worker. How about your bowling team or quilting group? Being with others gives one a level of comfort that might be difficult to reach otherwise. Sure, some may drop out after a visit or two, but if you find your passion, chances are that you'll stay on.

Volunteering with friends is a great way to get involved. Ocean City, Maryland, is a beach town with a winter population of less than 10,000 but which swells to over 300,000 on any summer weekend. During that peak season, most residents have little time for community service. When the tourists head back to the big city, a group of twelve friends get together to plan for their annual American Cancer Society fundraiser. They have a lot of fun working together and helping a cause in which they believe.

Marsha Howarth is one of the volunteers. "Our individual reasons for participating in the organization of this event are varied, but one compelling reason is that we feel we can actually make a substantial contribution that is meaningful not only to us, as individuals, but also to the community at large."

This chapter has described a wide variety of ways to get involved in volunteerism. Whether you are seven or seventy, there are boundless opportunities awaiting you. Making the commitment is the first step; defining how you will volunteer is the next.

Experience Corps Volunteers

The teacher and her aide were holding their own when the volunteers entered the classroom. The kids' eyes lit up as they saw their Experience Corps volunteers, and a few couldn't contain themselves as they ran up to hug them. At the Anderson Open School, in Minneapolis, Joycelyn Swanson, Frank G. Dye, Sr., and Val Jackson are retirees who volunteer at least fifteen hours per week reading to children.

They all took different routes to get there. Joycelyn joined AARP and listened to a presentation by an AmeriCorps representative. She decided to call and signed up. Frank babysat his grandchildren after becoming disabled. He answered a phone call for his son and he decided to attend the parents' meeting instead. He felt tied to the community where his grandchildren attended school and started volunteering. "I went to school near here, and now, sixty-one years later, I'm back." Val's daughter was looking for something for him to do in retirement and committed him to a stint at Seniors for Schools. He agreed to sign on for a year. That was seven years ago, and he is now more committed than ever.

Experience Corps Volunteers Val Jackson, Joycelyn Swanson, and Frank
G. Dye, Sr.

Their interaction with the kids showed without words that the love they had given them was reciprocated in full. Talking with them revealed how much their lives have been affected by these children. Joycelyn shared her thoughts: "It was just what I needed. I had been retired. It was a Godsend for me. I worked and learned a lot but never did what I wanted to do until now. I didn't think I'd like working with kids, but I do like it. They're smarter than you'd think. People I know are impressed with what I'm doing. If they are interested, I'll help them make the connection."

All of them are guilty of buying things for the kids when nobody is looking. Frank derives great joy from his time with them. "It's rewarding just to see a kid learn how to read. We give kids stickers when they succeed, and we give them stickers when they don't. We get as much out of it as the kids." Jamaican-born Val always wears a tie. One boy asked him, "What is that?" Val bought him a tie and shirt. Another boy wanted one also, so Val gave him one, too.

Frank G. Dye, Sr., and friends at the Anderson Open School in
Minneapolis

For volunteering their time, they receive a small stipend that mostly helps pay for gas and parking. Joycelyn summed it up, "This is like a pension. It helps. I like what I'm doing, and if I were rich, I'd do it anyway."

3

Defining Where You Will Volunteer

One of the considerations in volunteering is location. Most opportunities will involve going to a place outside your home. Some will be around the corner, and some on the other side of the world. There are even possibilities for involvement that do not require leaving home at all.

ON-SITE VOLUNTEERING

The vast majority of volunteer opportunities involve going to a location outside your home. For some this means working in the nonprofit office along with paid staff to get the job done, but most hands-on opportunities, whether driving a van, reading to children, or restoring wetlands, require some travel. Before committing to a volunteer opportunity, it is important to ask where you have to go and then determine how you are going to get there. If you require public transportation, make sure that it is available on the day and time of your volunteer service.

A rewarding way to volunteer outside of your home is to join the struggle against what we call the "scourge of loneliness," and there are many ways you can help. Loneliness, a powerful emotional experience, is characterized by a feeling of disconnection from a personal support network. Usually individuals experiencing emotional loneliness report that they have no one in whom they can trust and on whom they can rely. This particular circumstance seems to be experienced far more frequently by our senior citizens than it is by any other demographic group.

We believe the problem of loneliness is an extremely important one. If it were a disease, it would be our worst killer. It is usually not listed along with other social ills, such as hunger and poverty, and it often falls below the civic and community radar, yet here is a perfect area where volunteers of all ages can make a vital difference in the lives of others.

Today, due to the three Ds of social statistics (death, divorce, and deferred marriage), about one in every four households consists of a single person. If current trends continue, sociologists predict that the ratio will increase to one in every three households sometime during the twenty-first century.

Millions of us lead solitary lives, especially our elder citizens. For most, it is not by choice. The lives of many would be immeasurably enhanced by something as simple as a visit by a volunteer. In some cases, the lonely people themselves can become volunteers. By matching solitary individuals with others, we can give more meaning to all of their lives. For example, by providing opportunities for lonely elders to read to children, we can address multiple needs.

Another way to combat loneliness is by joining an animal sheltering organization. Local humane societies have clearly shown that the companionship of an animal is life enhancing and health renewing. Tony LaRussa is the manager of the St. Louis Cardinals. He and his wife, Elaine, founded the Animal Rescue Foundation (ARF), whose founding purpose was to find caring homes for abandoned companion animals. Since then, ARF's mission has expanded to include bringing the healing touch of animals to people in need. Over the past dozen years the foundation has witnessed the joy that these animals bring to the lives of the handicapped and lonely.

Tony is vitally committed to the work being done by ARF and its volunteers. "When Elaine and I started this project, it was primarily out of a concern for animals that had been mistreated or abandoned. We wanted to provide homes for them where they would be welcomed and loved. As we expanded our mission to match the needs of animals with people, greater benefits started to accrue. The effect that an animal brings to someone whose existence is largely solitary cannot be easily measured. We continue to witness the incredible changes that animals and people can bring to each other." Organizations such as ARF use volunteers in many different ways, such as animal care, animal adoption, education, office administration, and delivery of pet food and supplies.

Given increasing life expectancies, and as greater numbers of people become seniors, loneliness will be a social issue of far greater significance. Volunteer programs will have to become more innovative to serve seniors' needs and will have to include lonely people in the solutions to the problem.

VIRTUAL VOLUNTEERING

Virtual volunteering is a great way to offer your time and energies without leaving your home or place of business. A rapidly increasing number of nonprofits are offering online volunteer work. Also known as "cyber service," "online mentoring," and other inventive terms, virtual volunteering allows people to become involved who otherwise might not due to physical constraints, obligations at home, or a variety of other reasons.

The Virtual Volunteer Project was developed by ServiceLeader.org to facilitate the use of the Internet in volunteerism. Its Web site provides a good checklist for the potential volunteer and reinforces the notion that, as in any form of volunteering, a commitment to completing one's assignment should be taken seriously. Online mentoring, or "teletutoring," is an important component of its program, and anyone interested in teaching, but who has difficulty getting around, should give this a look.

The FYBR (Follow the Yellow Brick Road) pilot program is a first-of-its-kind web-based telementoring program. It matches business community, public sector, and individual volunteer telementors with youths who live in impacted areas. The FYBR goals are to improve workforce readiness skills in youth and to achieve greater quantity and quality of mentoring than is possible with in-person matches.

Best Buddies International is dedicated to enhancing the lives of people with intellectual disabilities by providing opportunities for one-to-one friendships and integrated employment. One of its programs, e-Buddies, seeks to fulfill the mission of Best Buddies by facilitating e-mail friendships between those who have intellectual disabilities and peers who do not. Individuals are matched in e-mail friendships based on age, gender, geography, and similar interests. Participants must commit to the program for one calendar year, during which time they will e-mail their match once a week. e-Buddies provides individuals with intellectual disabilities an opportunity to develop new friendships while acquiring much-needed computer skills.

Virtual volunteer opportunities such as these can be found at a number of Web sites, including www.servenet.org, www.volunteermatch.org, www.netaid.org, and others. You can use your skills as a grant writer, graphic arts designer, mentor or other talent to volunteer over the Internet.

VACATION VOLUNTEERING

There is a growing trend to combine travel or vacationing with service. Many are finding that there is more to a vacation than visiting this museum and that monument as the primary objective of travel.

Chuck Morlock was an English teacher in the Chicago area for thirty-four years. In many summers during those years, he went backpacking. About ten years ago, he decided to combine his passion for backpacking with an opportunity to give back. He found inexpensive trips sponsored by the American Hiking Society whose purpose was to work on a project, such as building a footbridge over a creek or restoring a trail. Volunteers spend a week to ten days in the wilderness with people who love the wilderness as much as they do. Most of the people are forty to seventy years old. This type of volunteering provides a great opportunity to share time with others. Volunteers join in the cooking, work on the projects, and sit around the campfire until it is time to sleep. Chuck's experiences keep him coming back. "It's a wonderful way to give back and see something concrete at the end of the week. Most of the stuff we build is going to be there for a while."

One of the trips included a family from New York City, a psychiatrist and psychologist, along with their daughter. They did not own a car, so they took the train to Utah, sleeping in a tent for the first time. Chuck reports that a lot of volunteers are in their sixties and even seventies. "People work to their limits, and that is entirely fine. Some people have even left in the middle after finding it wasn't their cup of tea."

For one considering this type of work, Chuck suggests doing something local at first. In local areas there may be clean-up projects or trail-restoration groups. The benefits of this type of volunteering include a good physical workout and the chance to be outdoors. Another benefit is the opportunity to meet other people with the same interests. Chuck said that he'll continue to contribute to these projects as long as he is able.

VolunteerAmerica connects individuals, families, and groups with volunteer opportunities and volunteer vacations on public lands all across America. It connects with Wilderness Volunteers, the Student Conservation Association, the Sierra Club, Landmark Volunteers, and others to provide numerous possibilities for getting outside and preserving our natural heritage.

Chuck Morlock helping to create a trail while on a volunteer vacation

Global Volunteers has been active for over twenty years, providing community-development projects worldwide. For those interested in international travel, Global Volunteers conducts service projects in child care, tutoring, English teaching, conservation work, health care, and construction/repair. It can also connect you domestically. You can help by painting and renovating homes in Metcalfe, Louisiana, working on a conservation project on the Blackfoot Reservation in Browning, Montana, or helping to organize a youth center in Rosebud, South Dakota.

BUSINESS TRAVEL VOLUNTEERING

No matter where in the world you wish to travel, there are opportunities to combine your trip with your talents in a volunteer capacity. Volunteering may lend a terrific balance to the travel experience, and as long as you are there, it may be easy to tack on a few extra days. Julie McCormack designs trips for Worldwide Escapes. She told us, "It places things in perspective for those of us who travel frequently on the company dollar, staying in five-star hotels that could easily cost as much per night as many locals earns in a month. Perhaps more importantly, volunteering gives travelers unique insight into the real situation in the countries to which they travel. Foreign companies often have their offices in the most posh areas of a city, and business travelers are put up in high quality hotels—both of which shield them from how many of the local residents live." She then listed a number of organizations who would love to put you to work, for a few days to much longer. Global Volunteers, the Red Cross, Oxfam, and the International Executive Service Corps are but a few.

CORPORATE VOLUNTEER PROGRAMS

Another way to get involved is through your workplace. A growing number of businesses are realizing the benefits of getting their employees involved with the community as volunteers. When employees volunteer, everyone wins. The business, whether large or small, is seen as contributing to more than its own bottom line.

Barb Alfrey is the manager for volunteer programs at General Mills Corporation. She described the beneficial nature of corporate programs. "General Mills gets a lot of positives out of it. It gets employees who are committed to the company because the company cares about the community. It is a real help in recruitment. It helps with employee development. People can develop skills during volunteering that they might not in their regular jobs, and they come back better.

Employees who volunteer have a stronger affiliation with the company, make a greater investment in the company, and are more likely to stay within the company and have greater skills."

Terry Clelen, who is the specialist in community involvement for Portland General Electric, recounts the success of its programs in 2002, estimating that about 55 percent of its employees volunteered. "Our multifaceted program used 2,774 volunteer employees and the total, with family members, was 3,273, which amounted to more than 105,000 hours. This equals 1.6 million dollars in donated time."

Terry describes some of the personal benefits associated with volunteering, emphasizing that employee volunteer programs help people discover their passion. "It is good for morale, working side by side with someone in a different capacity. It evens things out. Many volunteer activities are family oriented; they get the kids involved. For example, a beach clean up can be educational. In addition to the actual clean up, there can be a lesson in ecology. We encourage organizations to talk about what volunteers are doing and why they are doing it."

Participants often recognize that they have talents that can be transferred to the volunteer community. "There is something for everybody out there and everybody has something to contribute," Terry says.

Each corporate program may be unique to that business. Some provide release time so employees are paid for their volunteer hours during the workday. Others provide financial assistance to nonprofits based on the volunteer hours of their employees. There are many different ways of stimulating volunteer efforts, and more and more businesses see this as a part of their civic responsibility. If your business does not have such a program, you may want to encourage the idea. Business Strengthening America, an arm of the U.S. Chamber of Commerce, is a peer-to-peer business campaign working to encourage more Americans to serve in their communities. The Points of Light Foundation has developed *Principles of Excellence for Workplace Volunteering* as a guide to help employers of all sizes develop and implement employee volunteer programs that are fully integrated with business values.

SERVING ON A BOARD OF DIRECTORS

A great way to volunteer is to serve on the board of directors of a nonprofit organization. Generally, board members are selected because they bring business, organizational or programmatic skills to the leadership of the organization in addition to a passion for the mission. Many board members are recruited directly by an organization without having volunteered in other programs. Others have started out as non-board member volunteers and joined the board later. Pat spends a lot of his time at one of the Habitat for Humanity sites in San Francisco. He saw its public service announcement on a bus and called to volunteer, something he now does four to six days per week. He became so involved that he now serves on the board of directors of the local organization as well. For many nonprofits that do not have other volunteer programs, board membership is the only option for volunteers. There are about 860,000 nonprofits in the United States. If you multiply that number by five, the average number of board members for each organization, there are approximately 4,300,000 board members in America. Many of us know people who are board members of nonprofit organizations. Perhaps you are one already.

David Hudnut of Tiburon, California had served on a variety of boards and suggests two criteria for board service: enthusiasm and capability. Capability can mean many things—being able to contribute financially, possessing special occupational skills, and being able to work with others in forming a consensus about policy issues. There are a few things to consider, however, before making the commitment.

Charlene Harvey of San Francisco has been involved with boards for many years, both as a consultant and as a board member. She shared her perspective with us: "There are two types of volunteers, those who will do best on boards and those involved in the field programs of the nonprofit. One should examine how his or her personal strengths are best used. Be prepared to be tough, to ask tough questions, such as, *Should the organization merge with another nonprofit?* As a board member, you represent a number of areas, such as the IRS, donors, foundations, and volunteers."

While board membership is not for everyone, the joy of volunteering can be experienced by developing and implementing successful policy. Jim Greene is a retired U.S. Navy rear admiral and chaired the board of the Henry's Fork Foundation during the 1990s. The foundation serves to protect and promote this vital watershed in Eastern Idaho. Jim said that the most satisfying part of his efforts was getting farmers to talk with fishermen about leaving some water in the river. "Historically, these conversations had not occurred." This seemingly simple activity, getting people with disparate interests together, has made a huge difference in the way people view resources in the region.

In addition to setting policy, an important component of board service is financial support of the nonprofit. Most board members are expected to make a significant financial contribution to the organization. This has been referred to as "board dues." Many nonprofits are very clear when interviewing potential board members and give them a dollar figure of the minimum amount expected from them annually. If you are considering board service, you may want to know how much of a contribution you will be expected to make. However, there are exceptions to this rule. Many nonprofits are striving for a more diversified board membership than in the past. In some instances, the resultant board would include people without the resources to make the contribution normally expected. Other boards may want members who will work on projects and may not rely on them for significant financial contributions.

A prominent CEO of a large international conservation organization says that any prospective board member he considers must either be a potentially large donor, know potentially large donors, or have the skills to be influential in the environmental world. For him, funding the organization, as well as having friends do so, is a critical part of being a board member. Remember that a nonprofit organization's lifeblood is fundraising, and who better to do it than your board of directors?

There are other skills, however, that organizations are looking for in board members. It is not uncommon to find one or two lawyers on a board. They can help the organization with legal issues. The same goes for accountants, who can provide their expertise at no charge as well. You will also find people who are respected in the community, as they lend credibility to the organization by their involvement. Finally, you have people who are simply committed, hard working, and terrific at getting things done. While the specific reasons you are asked to join a board may differ, the general reason is that you can help the cause.

Before joining a board, it is critical that you ask a few questions. The first question should be, "Why do you want me on your board?" Wally Haas, a former owner of the Oakland A's baseball team, is currently serving on eight boards. "No matter who you are, it is important when you are asked to be on a board to ask the members, 'What do you want of me?' If they cannot be specific, you may want to think twice. It's much better to be clear, honest, and open with an organization going in to a board relationship." Another question Wally considers is how much time will be involved. "Ask, 'How often does the board meet?' Even if you are passionate about its cause, if you can't give them the time they want, it may not work out. It is better to set the expectations early."

It's Not for Everybody

John Howe has been a volunteer for much of his adult life and has thoroughly enjoyed it. Several years ago, he was asked to join the board of a nonprofit that provides services for children overseas, an organization to which he is committed financially and emotionally. Yet, he is having misgivings about his role: "For me, being on a board, it's harder to see the results of what I do. If you go out, for example, with a hammer and nails, at the end of the day you see the results of what you've done. I worked with a local immigrant; at the end of a few months he could speak and read some English, partially because of my efforts. I may decide to go back to a more basic one-on-one level." John is simply being honest about what gives him the greatest rewards. Executive directors want committed board members and not bodies filling up chairs.

If you are considering board service, it is important to remain attached to the mission of the nonprofit. You should ask yourself the following questions:

1. Am I emotionally attached to the mission of the organization?

2. Do I know enough about the organization?

You should ask the organization:

1. Why do you want me on the board?

2. What is the time commitment? How long is the term of service and how often do we meet?

3. What is the financial commitment?

So far, you have considered how much time you have available and where you will be doing the volunteering. The next thing to consider is what you will be doing when you volunteer.

Dave Lathrop

Phoenix Youth at Risk occupies a nondescript yet clean building in the southwest corner of the city. It is the site of some extremely positive changes in how mentoring programs are run. Dave Lathrop has been involved with mentoring since college, where he was a Big Brother. After moving to Phoenix, he was asked to take a look at Phoenix Youth at Risk. He became deeply involved in their programs and now trains mentors. Unlike some programs, where a parent or guardian enrolls the kids, here the kids take the responsibility of enrolling themselves. The difference is powerful and the results are encouraging.

He spoke with us about dealing with mentors. "Get honest with them as well as with the youths, who both have to make a commitment. The success of the program is directly related to the training involved. We provide training every Wednesday night for two and a half months prior to a five-day camp. It's important that people do enough homework so that they know what they are doing."

"In previous years, 50 percent success was good. It's hard for the kids. They work on goals to change their lives. Now they approach 90 percent success. In the past, the success was tied to the strength of the mentor; now it is program driven." Providing opportunities for the mentors to get together in order to share their problems and successes is an important part of the program. Being a mentor can be tough and lonely work. Discussing your experiences with other mentors makes everyone feel connected. They get the chance to realize that a problem for one is usually a problem for all of them, and they return to the relationships better prepared and more optimistic."

Mentoring has made a big difference in Dave's life. "Mentoring has given me a feeling that I've made a difference in someone else's life. There is a certain amount of peacefulness that goes along with that. It has me constantly looking at who I am. I wouldn't run my business in an unethical manner. It gives me a higher level of integrity. I used to get upset a lot more, and now I have a pretty balanced life. My emphasis on making a lot of money is not what it used to be. Your priorities get straightened out pretty quickly."

4

Bringing Along Your Skills

While some of us want to do a volunteer activity totally unrelated to the tasks we do all day, many prefer to serve using their occupational skills. Perhaps you have developed a high level of knowledge and experience and want to share it. You may have been doing some of this all along by performing your occupational tasks pro bono, i.e., with no fee attached. Whether you are performing life-saving surgery or completing a tax return, this is a great way to volunteer. Depending upon your occupation, you may not think that the work you do every day could translate into a volunteer opportunity. There is a good chance that it does. No matter what your area of expertise, there are nonprofits that can put you to work. We call this "sector volunteering," and it may be the right fit for you.

Whether you are still employed or have retired, there are opportunities in your field.

HEALTHCARE PROVIDERS

Every area of healthcare delivery offers volunteer opportunities domestically as well as abroad. Many find this is a great way to see the world and meet and treat some of the people in it. Mike Anker is a retired endodontist from Schenectady, NY, with a healthy dose of wanderlust coursing through his veins. Ten years ago he answered an ad in a dental journal asking for volunteer dentists in Israel. That was the first of more than a dozen trips all over the world. His experiences have resulted in lifelong friendships with others. "In the countries that I've worked in, the appreciation—sometimes even the adulation—is palpable. It is the desire of humans in general to feel loved and appreciated, and when on these trips it is unequivocal."

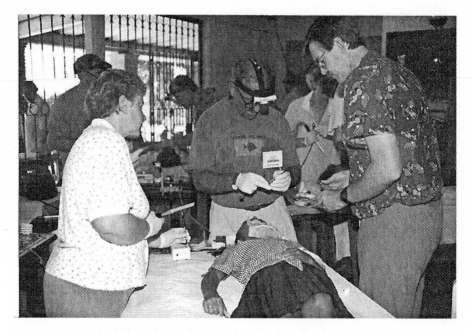

Dr. Mike Anker and team delivering dental care overseas

Mike has become a motivator/recruiter for others in health care and shares this message with his peers: "You've been given a gift of intelligence and education, and it would be a shame if some of it wasn't given back to people of lesser means."

The American Academy of Orthopaedic Surgeons is a sponsor of Orthopaedics Overseas, an arm of the international organization Health Volunteers Overseas. At one of its annual sessions, Dr. Bill Goodman of Pocatello, Idaho, was moved by its programs and signed on to go to Nepal for a month to teach local physicians and to perform orthopedic surgery at regional clinics. The commitment is a major one. Physicians, along with support staff—including nurses, nurse anesthetists, X-ray technicians, and lay staff—pay their own way to and from these distant sites, where a month is considered a minimum stay. In Nepal, Dr. Goodman performed surgeries for half-days, twice per week. He spent the balance of his time there teaching and seeing patients in the local clinics. On a recent trip to Peru, along with his wife Nancy, who is a nurse, and others, he saw hundreds of patients per day. Many of these people had trekked for four days through the Peruvian jungle to be seen.

One of his most memorable experiences was seeing a young girl receiving prosthetic arms. She had had both her arms chewed off above the elbows after falling into a pig pen at the age of eighteen months. Within fifteen minutes she was lifting small pieces of candy and feeding her family with her new arms, something that would take an adult many weeks to accomplish.

Bill looks at these opportunities as life altering, both for physicians as well as those who accompany them. "There is a big place for a nonprofessional to go along and just help, and an opportunity to see the world and go to a place that as a tourist they wouldn't ordinarily see. You get to see how the local people really live as well as extend a helping hand." He feels strongly that healthcare professionals should get involved. "Don't miss the opportunity. Seek it out and don't pass it up. This is one of the most satisfying, emotionally rewarding experiences that one can have in a professional lifetime."

TEACHERS AND TEACHING

It has often been said that the key to a more understanding and compassionate world is education. If you are a teacher, you put this philosophy into practice every day. While formal training in teaching is helpful, there are many volunteer opportunities for those without degrees in education. The ability to speak a second language is helpful but not a requirement for many of these programs. Opportunities for travel abound. Whether in a distant state or around the world, volunteer teachers are in great demand.

WorldTeach, i-to-i, TeachAbroad, and VolunteerAbroad are among dozens of organizations that provide opportunities to teach abroad, for periods ranging from two weeks to two years. In many cases you will be teaching English. In others you may be teaching in your own area of expertise, such as construction or conservation.

If you would rather stay in the U.S., your services will be welcomed all around the country. For example, the Inner City Teaching Corps places recent college graduates in inner-city Chicago schools. The University of Florida and the Institute of Food and Agricultural Services need volunteer teachers for their Cooperative Extension Service courses. Even dance teachers are asked to volunteer, for example, at the Regional High School Dance Federation event in Baltimore, Maryland.

If you want to teach, somebody wants you.

ACCOUNTANTS

Accountants can be helpful in many respects, and their volunteer efforts are in great demand. The Clearinghouse for Accounting Services provides assistance to nonprofits so they can make more dollars available for programs and expend less on administration. In Michigan, the Accounting Aid Society has 600 volunteers assisting in the preparation of tax returns for people living in poverty. It utilizes volunteers with expertise in accounting, law, business management, human resources, and other areas of nonprofit management. In Illinois, CPAs for the Public Interest provides similar services. It's likely that such an opportunity is available in your state as well.

Nationally, Accountants for the Public Interest (API) has twenty-two national affiliates, with over 10,000 volunteer accountants. Volunteers lend short-term technical assistance to nonprofits and small businesses, tax assistance to low-income individuals, and accountants for service on boards of directors of non-profit organizations.

ATTORNEYS

Many local bar associations provide pro bono legal opportunities for member attorneys. This is a great way for lawyers to utilize their training to assist low-income individuals. It's also an inspired method for dealing with that aspect of our culture known as "lawyer jokes."

The Office of the Child Advocate in the state of Delaware provides training and opportunities for pro bono work, ranging in periods from three months to over one year. Pro bono activities of the Orange County Bar Association include the Domestic Violence Project, the Grandparent/Guardianship Project, the Bankruptcy Project, and family law basic training. The latter provides training in family law issues, after which participants accept two pro bono cases from the public law center. Using volunteers, the Pro Bono Project of Santa Clara, California, offers access to high-quality legal representation in civil disputes to low-income people for cases in Santa Clara County courts.

Attorneys are valued members of boards of directors for obvious reasons, and most nonprofits are happy to have more than one.

YOUR OCCUPATION

No matter what you do, there are volunteer opportunities for practically every profession and job description imaginable. Builders without Borders, Architects without Borders, and Habitat for Humanity can all use your special knowledge and skills. A great organization is SCORE, the Senior Corps of Retired Executives, whose mission is to assist small businesses in their growth process. If you have knowledge in areas such as marketing, finance, sales, or operations, and want to remain involved in the working world, this may be the right place for you. Whatever your previous job, if you are interested in applying your skill set to a volunteer opportunity, there is an organization out there that will be happy to make your acquaintance.

One such opportunity exists in Minneapolis, where people are fortunate to have a place where they can go to get psychological counseling for free. Gary Schoener is the executive director of the Walk-In Counseling Center (WICC) and has been with it since its inception in 1969. WICC offers confidential services and pro bono counseling to members of the community while providing an extremely valuable environment for the therapists themselves. The volunteer counseling staff is probably the largest in the world, providing assistance to over 3,000 clients per year. How do they do it? Gary explains, "There is a rigorous screening, including interviews with previous supervisors, and personal interviews that include role playing. As you make the club more exclusive, more people want to join. Working here is a credential that helps people get jobs. Even board members do well because of their affiliation."

The WICC volunteer staff lists over 300 psychologists and clinical social workers, with over 200 involved in any calendar year. One of the keys for the volunteers is the concept of "supervision," or review by their peers. After each afternoon or nightly session, the counselors, along with a supervisor, gather to discuss the session's cases. "In the field, about one in ten visits are supervised. Here, 100 percent of the visits are reviewed, even those of the supervisors." This is the absolute best way for professionals to maintain their skills and learn from their colleagues.

"One of my favorite places is here. Some volunteers are new in town and it is a great way to connect," said Carol Oldowski, a nurse by training who has been volunteering at WICC for years. "The WICC offers a great opportunity to expand your skills. This program is unique."

Executive Director Gary Schoener outside the Walk-In Counseling Center

MENTORING

While not a specific profession, mentoring is a type of volunteering that draws on important interpersonal skills. The need for mentors is huge. According to the National Mentoring Partnership, approximately 35.2 million children aged ten to eighteen live in the United States. Of that number, about half—or 17.6 million—could benefit greatly from a high-quality formal mentoring relationship with a caring adult. Many face especially difficult circumstances: one out of four lives with only one parent; one out of ten is born to teen parents; one out of five lives in poverty; and many will not finish high school.

Currently, it is estimated that, of the 17.6 million young people who need mentors, approximately 2.5 million are in formal, high-quality mentoring relationships. That means more than 15 million young people still need mentors. The National Mentoring Partnership lists ten primary reasons why people don't become mentors or see the job through. Among the reasons are public fear and misconceptions about young people and mentoring.

Kari Davis is the executive director of the Mentoring Partnership of Minnesota. She was quick to point out that a major problem in retaining mentors is a lack of understanding regarding their role as mentors. Of primary importance: "Training, training, and training, followed by peer support and support training."

Kari is clear on what mentoring is all about. "A mentor is a friend, confidant, and cheerleader. Our goal is to give the kids skills to make decisions and encourage them in whatever decisions they make. You're not there to be a parent, to tell them what to do. If you train volunteers not to expect the impossible, for kids, it's life changing."

While mentoring teens seems daunting, Kari feels that it doesn't have to be. She likes working with those in high school. "For me, it's about having a passion for kids. They want to know who you are. Here are the boundaries—mentors can't exceed them. Teenagers are by nature going to question."

Kari explains that there are different expectations at different ages. "Mentoring works with teens because they expect adults to leave when things go wrong, but the mentors stay. Building trust is the first job. If you care about kids, it doesn't matter where you come from. They want to learn something. These kids are hungry to meet different people."

A problem with some mentoring programs is that the mentors feel alone and crave feedback from their peers. She feels that it is important to bring mentors together three to four times per year for peer counseling and support. "Use each other as a sounding board so that you create a network. You're going to make mistakes; it's okay, because you have support out there."

Mentors like Kari are performing remarkable services. They are on the front lines, changing people's lives while enhancing their own. If you are looking for the same kind of feeling, mentoring may provide that opportunity.

Whether you are interested in doing something related to your line of work or something totally different, the next step is to find the volunteer opportunity that is right for you.

John Bell

In the late 1970s there were only two hospice programs in the country. One of those was located near the home of John Bell, who runs a successful travel agency in Northern California. After attending a dinner for the Hospice of Marin, he was so impressed that he began to volunteer. Upon completing a six-month training program, John became the first lay volunteer to be given the opportunity to deal directly with patients. He developed a strong relationship with a patient, Robert J. Sturhahn, and after his death set up a foundation in his name. John's goal was to do something for children. He saw a TV show about a New York camp for cancer patients and approached Stanford University, UCSF, and other groups, all of whom had started to think about the same type of thing.

They combined resources to rent a Campfire Girls camp in the Sierra Nevada Mountains and hosted twenty-eight children for half a week. That was the beginning. As time passed, more kids were being diagnosed with cancer at the same time that survival rates were increasing, creating a much greater demand. The camp was falling apart physically. With the aid of campers' parents they attempted to make repairs. Following these efforts, they decided to have family weekends and then weekend sessions with siblings. This evolved into entire camping weeks for siblings. It became obvious that the program was going to be really big, and it was. The camp began to attract serious attention after John received the Jefferson Award in a ceremony at the White House.

They began to have increased fund-raising success and became the Okizu Foundation. Since then, they have gone from 28 to over 800 kids per summer, inviting 2,200 family members in total. They have two weekends for families whose children have died.

During the 1990s they simply ran out of room, and so they built their own camp near Oroville. At first they cooked at a school down the road and ate in a big tent. They have built an infirmary but have not had the money to furnish it with the equipment needed. Even now, nearly the entire staff, including the medical staff, is comprised of volunteers. At the camp, they routinely have about forty counselors, all of whom are volunteers, primarily college students. Volunteers also serve as guides for most of the activities. Of the counselors, at least fifteen are former campers or siblings.

John told us that currently one in four campers with cancer will die, but that it used to be one in two. We asked him what Camp Okizu has meant to him. "It has made the rest of my life completely harmonious, because I have no doubt about what is important in the world. If I weren't doing this camp, I'd have a lot more road rage. I'd be a lot more concerned about my 401(k)."

Feeling the love at Camp Okizu

Jefry Rosmarin

Jefry Rosmarin is a real estate developer on Long Island who has a habit of saving newspaper articles that capture his imagination. Many years ago he was moved by an article about businessman Gene Lang. In 1981, Lang returned to the elementary school he had attended fifty years earlier to give a speech to a class of graduating sixth graders. On the way to the podium, P.S. 121's principal told Lang that three-quarters of the school's students would probably never finish high school, prompting Lang to make an extraordinary impromptu change to his speech: He promised college tuition to every sixth grader who stayed in high school and graduated. Several years later he started the "I Have a Dream" Foundation, which encourages other successful men and women to make similar commitments.

Jefry saved the article. "I kept returning to it and I kept making excuses. Finally, I decided that it was time to do it." He wrote the "big check" and sponsored a group of students who had finished the fifth grade. "I reviewed some data and chose the area. There is as much need there as anywhere on Long Island. I could have gone to an area better for my business." If he thought it would be simple, he was mistaken. "If you put up a brass ring, you think they will grasp at it. It's not so easy." Like Lang, he became involved. "I like to roll up my sleeves. I meet with the students once a week."

About his involvement: "You're there one on one with the kids, and you hire the project coordinator." When asked about the challenges, he replied, "It's hard to develop a rapport. I come from a different culture and they're suspicious. I tried to engage the kids, but it's not always easy. They are thinking, 'What's your goal?' Now I'm starting to get some nice things—Christmas cards and thank-yous are starting to appear. We've also had some failures. Some of the biggest successes and biggest failures come from the same people. One girl had three kids but graduated high school and went to vocational school. Of the original group, 94 percent graduated from high school, compared with the normal 64 percent rate for the school. It has been frustrating but enormously satisfying. High school graduation was pretty neat. This year we should have some graduating college seniors."

Not one to watch from the sidelines, Jefry has since started a basketball mentoring program. "It is difficult to get volunteers for programs like this, but it is easier this way. On the basketball court the barriers are very low." Once he started this he called the "Dreamers" and asked them to get involved, and they have been active. The basketball program breaks the ice. "If you like it, you just come, and if you don't, you don't." According to Jefry, "You dip your toe in and then you're involved."

5

Finding the Volunteer Opportunity

So far you have answered many key questions about your volunteer potential. You've considered your age and whether you will be volunteering as an individual or with others, such as your spouse, family, or co-workers. You've thought about whether you will go to the volunteer site or work over the phone or Internet. You've considered whether you will volunteer using your occupational skills or branch out to other areas where you wish to try something different. You are probably asking yourself, "What do I do now?" Before you get on the phone or go on the Web, this is a great time to revisit and perhaps make some changes to the questions that you answered in Chapter 1.

THE "HOW CAN I SERVE BEST" QUESTIONNAIRE #2

Ask yourself the following questions (some are repeats):

1. What do I really have a passion for? _____

2. How much time can I realistically commit at this point in my life?

 Hours per week _____
 Hours per month _____

3. Type of Commitment

 a. _____ episodic (intermittent)
 b. _____ long-term
 c. _____ mega (a year or more)

For long-term or mega commitments, will I be available for training? _____

3. What type of job do I want?

    a. _____ hands-on
    b. _____ board of directors membership
    c. _____ virtual volunteering
    d. _____ administrative/office

4. I would rather

    a. _____ use my job or professional skills.
    b. _____ learn new skills different from my present job skills.
    c. _____ do a combination of both.

5. Who is going?

    a. _____ I'm volunteering as an individual.
    b. _____ I'm volunteering with my spouse.
    c. _____ I'm volunteering with my family.
    d. _____ I'm volunteering with a friend or group.
    e. _____ I'm interested in a group for singles.

6. Do I have an organization in mind? _____

    If so, which one? _____

7. How am I planning to connect?

    a. _____ phone
    b. _____ Internet
    c. _____ I need help connecting

8. What's holding me back?

_____

_____

Answering the questions will prepare you to make contact with a nonprofit. The two most important steps are to find your passion and to be honest about your available time. If you only have time available on an episodic basis or just want to test the volunteer waters, finding a volunteer opportunity can be relatively easy. If you have an organization in mind, give them a call or go to the Web site. Perhaps you have a sector in mind but not a specific organization. If you are using the

Internet, a little bit of surfing may reveal the outfit best suited to your interests. However, many of you will rely on more traditional means of making that first connection.

NOT USING THE INTERNET?

If you don't know where to go, you are not alone. The Pew Partnership is a civic research organization whose mission is to identify and document solutions and strategies that are crucial to strong communities. Its recently published survey of communities, entitled *Ready, Willing and Able: Citizens Working for Change*, provides strong insights into how people feel about where they live. "For those who did not volunteer…41 percent said they wanted to get involved in their community but didn't know how or whom to call." If you are not comfortable with the Internet or do not have access, a number of excellent methods remain for finding the right volunteer opportunity.

Ask a Friend—Still the Best Method

You probably have a number of friends who are active volunteers. Ask them about their experiences, their methods of connecting, and their opinions on the good and bad points of volunteering. They may be able to recommend a nonprofit with whom you can connect. You may even be able to tag along on their next volunteer date to get a better idea of what's involved and whether it is right for you.

Dave Perron, who is involved with CAPCURE (Association for the Cure of Cancer of the Prostate), says, "What organizations should do but don't is have volunteers recruit volunteers." So, if you find a nonprofit that looks promising, talk with some of the volunteers to find out how they are enjoying their experiences.

Your House of Worship

Many people, especially senior volunteers, connect through their houses of worship. There may be specific programs within the religious institution, or it may be able to recommend organizations in the community that can use your volunteer services.

Your Organizations

Many organizations have a nonprofit or volunteer component. Ask someone in the administrative office if any volunteer opportunities are available or if they can recommend a place to call or visit. An example is the AARP, which actively helps to connect people with nonprofits in search of volunteers.

Local Newspapers/Newsletters

Many newspapers list volunteer opportunities as a service to the community. Some list them daily while others may do so on weekends or on a specific day of the week. Most of these opportunities are short term, although longer term volunteer opportunities may be found.

Let Your Fingers Do the Walking

The phone book is impersonal, but it can be a great way to start. We did a little detective work, comparing the phone book to the Internet to see where we could find the most volunteer opportunities. Our random focus was on volunteer opportunities in literacy. In the front of our local phone book is a section listing all of the various community services. Beneath the "Education" heading were two numbers that we decided to call, the Marin County Office of Education and the Marin Literacy Program. Under the "Volunteer Programs" heading was the local volunteer center. We called each of them, and this is what we found.

Volunteer Centers

There are currently over 500 volunteer centers in the U.S. They can be found in all of the major population areas and in a huge number of smaller ones. Volunteer centers are clearinghouses for a wide variety of nonprofit organizations. After you call or visit them and describe your interests, they will likely be able to connect you with an organization that will match up well with your desires and skills. The center in our area is called the Center for Volunteer and Nonprofit Leadership of Marin, and it offers volunteer opportunities for dozens of nonprofits. A call to its volunteer services coordinator resulted in a prompt reply offering opportunities for both adults and children in the Marin Literacy Program, the Marin Conservation Corps, the Marin Community Clinic, the San Rafael Canal Ministry, and the Canal Community Alliance.

County Office of Education
It should be easy to find the number of the local school district, perhaps even by calling the schools in your neighborhood. Schools are eager for volunteers who can assist children in developing reading skills, and all have their individual programs and requirements for volunteers. We called the Marin County Office of Education and were directed to the Marin County School Volunteers office. The office was very helpful and described programs that ran both during and after school. It screens, trains, and places the volunteers. We made a total of two calls, and we received information about the program in the next day's mail.

Marin Literacy Program
We left a message and received a call the next day describing its library-based programs, which match volunteers with adult students. It actively recruits tutors yet never seems to have enough. It has monthly one-and-a-half hour orientation sessions, followed by two consecutive all-day Saturday training sessions. Volunteers are then matched with students.

The phone is an easy yet powerful way to connect with nonprofits, and in this day and age it is nice to actually speak with a person. A few minutes spent on the phone can result in a wide variety of choices. Remember, you have the option to choose what you want to pursue.

USING THE INTERNET

If you are comfortable "surfing the net," it will be easy to find multiple Web sites offering volunteer opportunities. If you are new to the Internet or do not feel comfortable performing a search, there are a few places you can go where you should find it easy to make connection with a nonprofit in your area of interest. Don't be discouraged if one site refers you to a second site, or even a third. For example, if you go to the Points of Light Foundation's Web site, it will connect you with the volunteer center in your area, and from there you will be able to find individual volunteer opportunities locally. We will discuss a number of Web sites in this chapter. For a more thorough list, see Appendix A.

It should be noted that several hundred Web sites are mentioned in this book. Those pertaining to specific nonprofits were found randomly during the writing of the book. Hundreds of thousands of terrific organizations exist, and most have Web sites. Our purpose is to teach you about the process involved in finding them, not to recommend any specific nonprofits for your involvement. As mentioned earlier, you are the one setting the priorities.

A Little Surfing Music

By connecting with one of the Web sites listed below, or in the Appendix, you may find just the volunteer opportunity you are looking for. You may also find your way to other useful Web sites during your browsing. Be prepared to spend a little time searching if you do not have a specific organization in mind. It would be great if there were more sector-oriented Web sites, such as www. earthshare.org, which has links to environmental groups offering volunteer opportunities, but these are somewhat rare. Once you have found something that looks promising, you may want to check out the nonprofit's Web site to see if the organization is one you would like to join. If it is a one-time volunteer opportunity, you may not be as curious as if you are volunteering for a long-term commitment. Use the guidelines listed in the next chapter to evaluate the nonprofit organizations you find.

One useful way to find an opportunity is to use a search engine, such as Google www.google.com or Yahoo www.yahoo.com, looking for organizations specific to your area of interest. Continuing our search for volunteer opportunities in literacy, we did just that.

A Web search for "literacy" produced the National Center for Family Literacy, at www.famlit.org. This site can connect you with a family literacy program in your area. It also provides a phone number, 1-877-FAMLIT-1.

Another site we found was the Literacy Volunteers of America, at www. literacyvolunteers.org. This site connected us with the Marin Literacy Program, cited earlier in this chapter.

Among the dozens of Web sites providing volunteer information, there were a few that were exceptional when it came to offering short-term or episodic opportunities. We visited several volunteer clearinghouse sites looking for opportunities to teach literacy. We found the following:

- VolunteerMatch www.volunteermatch.org: When we visited this site we typed in "literacy" and our zip code. It listed not only the Marin County School Volunteers but other possibilities as well, such as the After-School Study Center, which assists teens with homework, and the Library Outreach program, which takes books to seniors unable to get to and from the library.

- The Points of Light Foundation www.pointsoflight.org: This site connected us with the local volunteer center. A search of this site revealed the
Marin Community Clinic, which offers opportunities to read to children
aged two to six.

Surfing the Internet has become a national pastime and millions have become
skillful at it. Appendix A provides more information about a number of organizations, both government and private, whose Web sites may be useful to you. For
those interested in finding volunteer opportunities via the Web, our suggestion to
you is, "Just do it."

A WORD OF CAUTION

When considering volunteering for an organization, or even donating money to
one, heed this cautionary note. Anyone using the Internet should be aware that
fake Web sites exist. If you find an organization that looks good but that you
haven't heard of, it should be possible to find out more about them. The first
thing that you can do is call. Then we recommend following the guidelines listed
in the next chapter. Next, go to www.guidestar.com, which contains the recent
financial statements of the majority of nonprofits. Some valuable information can
be found in Appendix C, which addresses the issue of how to be comfortable
when you make a financial contribution, but which also applies to making a volunteer commitment.

The next chapter provides guidelines for evaluating volunteer opportunities, as
well as more information about nonprofits.

Charlie Garfield

In describing why he changed careers while in his early twenties, Dr. Charles Garfield explained, "I decided that I wanted my life's work to be more about the heart than the mind." At age twenty-three, Charlie Garfield was already a successful mathematician, a computer analyst, and an integral part of the Apollo 11 lunar module team, which would successfully land the first man on the moon. Despite the excitement of the lunar project and a potentially brilliant career ahead of him, he decided that it would be more fulfilling to "work more with people than with technology." When asked if this was a tough decision, Charlie said no, it was the only decision he could have made. He left the space program and went back to school for a graduate degree in psychology. After graduating, he decided to write his post-doctoral thesis on cancer patients to try to analyze and understand the psychology of cancer victims and cancer survivors. Like the people he had worked with on Apollo 11, cancer survivors were mission driven.

Throughout many interviews with cancer victims, Charlie became entranced by the stories of how they and their families were coping with terminal illness. He was profoundly affected by these meetings and especially their desire to have someone to talk to during their ordeal. "I decided that nobody should ever have to die alone." He felt that support groups for cancer patients needed to be established. He called thirty friends and associates and asked them to join him in this endeavor. On an evening in 1974, fifteen people joined Charlie to meet about his idea. That evening, the Shanti Project was born.

In addition to serving hospice patients, including those afflicted with cancer and AIDS, the Shanti organization is the most widely used volunteer training model in the world. To date, it has trained 600 organizations in volunteer management, while another 1,000 organizations have been trained by the Shanti National Training Institute. The Shanti model incorporates the best management concepts in the business world and applies them to nonprofits. Charlie believes that while a lot can be learned from the business practices of corporations, the for-profit world can actually learn more from their nonprofit counterparts. He feels that good practices and procedures can be articulated on paper and learned but that the strengths in the nonprofit world, such as compassion and ethics, are more intangible and tougher to learn. These training programs have been published and are accessible throughout the world for nonprofits to use. Dr. Garfield believes that good training of volunteer staffs is critical to organizations that serve.

He says that for the volunteer, "Finding a volunteer commitment is like falling in love." While people volunteering for the first time may feel some anxiety, the chance to serve will quickly overcome those feelings. "It is a sublime pleasure to volunteer. None of the wisdom traditions have any notions of materialism, such as needing to bust your butt to buy a Mercedes. Picture, though, an audience of prospective volunteers who twenty-five years from now say to themselves, 'Thank God I discovered volunteering, because it has brought such meaning to my life.'"

6

Evaluating the Nonprofit and the Volunteer Opportunity

Whether you find your volunteer opportunity via the phone, Internet, or a conversation with Aunt Maude, you are going to want to know more. How much you want or need to know about the nonprofit depends upon whether you are a one-timer, an on-going, or a mega-committer.

ONE-TIME OR INTERMITTENT VOLUNTEERING

If you are participating on a one-time or episodic basis, while it is nice to know details, you may not want to engage in extensive research about the nonprofit. If you find the opportunity through one of the national clearinghouses, it is likely that the organization has been checked out by the group sponsoring the Web site and that it is for real. For example, VolunteerMatch receives inquiries from several dozen new groups every day that it will screen and approve before adding them to its listings. While the first opportunity you choose may not be the best fit for you, the experience should at least be a learning one. You may want to do a bit more research before undertaking the next opportunity.

ONGOING AND "MEGA-VOLUNTEERING"

There is a significant difference between this type of commitment and one-time or intermittent volunteering. Both you and the nonprofit are committing to each other, so you need to be relatively sure that the organization is right for you, especially if you are planning to participate with an international organization and spend a significant time abroad. If you are considering becoming a mentor, an adequate training program is essential before you meet your mentee. You should do a significant amount of research before you commit.

The following overview will give you a better idea about how the nonprofit is structured.

NONPROFIT STRUCTURE

Tax-Exempt Status

Nonprofit organizations are characterized by their special tax-exempt status granted by the Internal Revenue Service, the same organization that suggests otherwise when considering your personal tax return. Not-for-profit organizations that qualify are granted tax exemption and are listed as 501(c) corporations. Most are designated 501(c)(3) entities, and your financial contributions to them are tax deductible. Currently, there are over 860,000 qualifying nonprofit organizations.

Governance

Nonprofits usually have a board of directors, executive director, paid staff, volunteer staff, and program volunteers.

Board of directors: Each nonprofit has a board of directors that determines the direction and activities of the organization. Generally, its job is to set policy, and its members have a duty to oversee the operations of the organization. Depending upon the size of the entity, the board may consist of a handful of members, while many larger organizations have twelve to sixteen members or more on their boards. A board president or chairperson acts in a leadership capacity. Board members are generally unpaid and are selected for a variety of reasons. All board members are expected to make some financial contribution and to become involved in the fundraising aspects of the nonprofit. Members who bring balance to the board of directors are desired so that the nonprofit can accomplish its mission in a cost-effective manner that represents the broader interests of the community.

Executive director: Each nonprofit has someone in charge of its daily activities, usually designated its executive director (ED). This is usually a salaried position, and the ED is chosen by the board of directors and is responsible to them. The

ED and his/her staff carry out the policy of the board of directors. Organizations work best when there is close communication between the board chairperson and the ED. However, the board should allow the ED to carry out its programs without trying to micromanage and involve themselves with the day-to-day activities of the staff.

Paid staff: The paid staff plays a large role in the effectiveness of the nonprofit sector. Historically, these have not been the highest paying jobs in the workforce. Yet many people choose to work for nonprofits because they want to make a difference, and most are passionate about the organization for which they serve. Far too many of us go to work each day either loathing or at best feeling uninspired about our jobs. A far higher percentage of nonprofit staff members truly feel that their work is important and actually enjoy what they do.

Many nonprofits have created the position of volunteer coordinator, or some equivalent, whose job is to create and manage meaningful volunteer programs. A large number of small nonprofits would love to have such a position but cannot justify it financially. Volunteer coordinators may provide training themselves or recruit and coordinate trainers for their volunteers. Former board chairman Jim Greene gave us a general rule that for organizations whose budgets are up to one million dollars, there is one staff position per $100,000 of revenue. A huge number of 501(c)(3) organizations fit into this category, and many simply cannot justify a salaried volunteer coordinator position. Often this role is handled by a staff member with other duties or shared among several paid staff. Do not give up on an organization if it doesn't have a volunteer coordinator, especially if it has a relatively small staff.

Volunteer staff: Many people join the volunteer staff of nonprofits as their way of supporting the organization. Volunteer staff often have flexible schedules, which enable them to contribute their time more easily. Volunteers often perform duties that allow the paid staff more time to focus on its mission and accomplish the goals of the nonprofit. Many nonprofits would be hard-pressed to function without such volunteer effort.

How Nonprofits Work

Nonprofits employ a variety of written documents. In addition to qualifying for tax-exempt status, the nonprofit has or should have additional written materials such as a mission statement, perhaps a vision statement, a strategic plan, an annual report, a financial statement, and other evaluative data that tells how effective it has been in fulfilling its mission.

The first thing that characterizes a nonprofit is that it was created to fulfill a need identified by the person or persons who started it. This need and the goals it sets to meet it are articulated in the form of a mission statement. Many mission statements are one-liners. Others are long, sprawling mandates. If you are considering volunteering, it is important that the ideas presented in the mission statement be meaningful and relevant for you.

Here are some examples of mission statements:

Trout Unlimited's mission is to conserve, protect, and restore North America's trout and salmon fisheries and their watersheds.

The American Cancer Society is the nationwide community-based voluntary health organization dedicated to eliminating cancer as a major health problem by preventing cancer, saving lives, and diminishing suffering from cancer through research, education, advocacy, and service.

The mission of the Literacy Volunteers of America is to change lives through literacy.

Heifer International's mission: To work with communities to end hunger and poverty and care for the earth.

To meet these lofty goals, organizations need direction. This is partly the purpose of the strategic plan. Many nonprofits create working documents that direct their activities for a specified period of time, for example three, five, or ten years. The strategic plan is often the result of the combined efforts of the executive director, the staff, the board of directors, the volunteers, and perhaps a consultant versed in the field. The plan defines the mission and vision of the nonprofit and proposes activities that will move the organization toward its intended goals. The strategic planning process is a valuable step, making sure that all involved are headed in the same direction. Perhaps the mission has been too broad for the nonprofit to accomplish. Perhaps the needs of its constituency have changed and the group needs to reassess its goals. Perhaps the mission is obsolete or the goals are best served by another group. Maybe it is time for the nonprofit to consider a strategic merger with another organization or to close its doors altogether. Strategic plans should include methods for evaluating the success or failure in achieving the nonprofit's mission. The planning process can be incredibly liberating to the organization; it can help it re-evaluate its goals and mechanisms for assessing its effectiveness. Planning helps infuse new life into a nonprofit that may have lost its way.

An annual report is another tool for evaluating a nonprofit's progress. It is a succinct way of letting those concerned see just what has been done during the past year. What projects are ongoing and what projects have been completed? What is the financial status of the nonprofit? How many volunteers are working for the organization, and where do we need more? These and other questions can be answered in an annual report, which speaks to the "state of the nonprofit." It need not be extensive, but it should serve to educate those interested in the entity.

Just as in the "real world," financial statements are necessary, and honest ones are mandatory. A nonprofit will have, among other financial statements, a balance sheet and an income statement. The balance sheet lists assets and liabilities and, hopefully, a positive bottom line. The income statement shows financial trends over time and can show if the organization is headed in the right direction financially. An audit is another source of information for those who may want to contribute financially or volunteer time and energy.

In order to assess the effectiveness of an organization in achieving the goals set forth in the mission statement and strategic plan, there should be evaluations of the job being done. Organizations should ask themselves if they are working toward their mission. If so, what data is there that shows its effectiveness? If they are in the business of treating injured animals, how many have successfully been treated, how many are in the process of being treated, and how many have not recovered or have died? If their work is in the field of literacy, how many people have been taught to read? Have they been able to find better employment opportunities? Have they been able to pass appropriate examinations? If not, why not? Maybe the process of education is inappropriate; perhaps the educational tools are obsolete. Maybe the venue at which services are provided is not conducive to learning. Perhaps a language barrier exists. These and many other questions should be raised as part of the continuing process of evaluation and should be welcomed by the organization and not feared. How are organizations to improve if they don't ask questions and actively seek the answers?

Any nonprofit worth your time, energy, and possible financial support should be able to provide written materials describing its activities, means of support, goals, and effectiveness in achieving its goals. If you are volunteering for a long-term commitment, you should expect to have your questions answered. If the organization is not forthcoming, you may want to look elsewhere for the volunteer opportunity that is right for you.

WHAT'S NEXT?

We have just described the general structure and organization of nonprofits. After finding what may be a great opportunity, you'll probably want to learn a bit more about the specific nonprofit organization. Here are some suggestions for learning more about the organization and the volunteer opportunity it offers.

Visit the Agency
In many instances, the nonprofit will have an office near you. Pay them a visit. If possible, speak with the executive director, who will usually be seen moving around at the speed of light. Speak with the staff. Ask them why they choose to work there. If they seem passionate about what they are doing, you may have found the right spot. You may be able to watch other volunteers in action. The best way to learn about any organization is to talk with those who have already made a commitment. By being on site, you can get a fair idea of how the organization works and if your talents can meld with its services.

Obtain Literature about the Organization
Nonprofits describe themselves in written materials. Obtain brochures plus any other available literature. While much of what you read will be geared to fundraising efforts, you should get a good feel for what the nonprofit does and the constituency it serves.

Speak with the Volunteer Coordinator
If the organization you are interested in has a volunteer coordinator, the chances are good that a lot of thought has gone into how to utilize your contribution. Ask them what opportunities are available and to whom you would be reporting. If the agency does not have a volunteer coordinator, this should not be held against them for reasons already stated. All that matters is that the organization has put time and effort into developing meaningful volunteer opportunities.

Visit The Web site
Almost every organization with two people or more has a Web site these days. Look the nonprofit up on the Internet and learn about what it does and why.

Evaluate The Mission Statement
A great place to start your evaluation is to focus on the mission statement. Watch out for mission statements that are too broad. For example, if an organization has

as its mission statement, "To feed the homeless," perhaps it is not as focused as it should be. The mission statement of the Food Pantry in Healdsburg, California, is "To provide food for migrant workers in Sonoma County that are below the poverty line." This is a more specific and tangible mission statement.

Look for Outcomes

An impressive mission statement means little if the agency is not performing. This performance is referred to as "outcomes." The best organizations are those that are able to measure success. Almost all of the large foundations today require that the organizations they support are able to measure outcomes and successes.

Talk with Board Members

Take a look at the list of those serving on the board of directors. If you know one of them, call and ask why he or she became involved. Find out if his or her expectations going in have been met and what the frustrations are. Find out how involved the board is in the organization. Some boards are less engaged in the operations, while others are actively involved. With which agency would you rather become involved? Beware of the organization that exhibits significant tension between the board and staff.

Ask about Training

Many long-term volunteer opportunities require training. This benefits you, the organization, and the people it serves. Training is a two-way street, where both you and the organization show a responsibility to each other. Expect to attend one or more training sessions, depending upon the activity for which you are planning to serve.

By learning about the nonprofit and its programs you will be able to get a feel for whether or not you will be appropriate for each other. Now that you have a good feeling about a nonprofit and are considering joining, you must next define your expectations. This is the focus of the next chapter.

Steve Perry

The rock group Journey was on the top of the charts for a great deal of the seventies and eighties, and Steve Perry was their lead singer. Their popularity led to performances all over the world, with all of the highs and lows that characterize rock stardom. Staying grounded is not an easy thing to do when hordes of people idolize you, captivated by the aura of musical excitement. Steve is one of the rare individuals who uses his rock stardom to benefit society, meeting with the terminally ill.

Since 1980, the Make-A-Wish Foundation has been granting the wishes of children with life-threatening medical conditions. "One of the prerequisites, an absolute must for me, is that no publicity is brought to this. In my heart of hearts, I know that my reason for doing it was just to complete this person's last wish. It wasn't about publicity.

"There was a sixteen-year-old boy in Ohio with cystic fibrosis who was supposed to come out here to watch Journey rehearse. He became too ill to travel, so we took an overnight flight and went to his bedside. The nurse warned us that even though he was sixteen he looked smaller and younger. He was sedated and comfortable when we arrived. It hit me in a way that I was unprepared for. He opened his eyes and looked around the room at the group and his eyes got big, and then the sedation took over and he closed them. We placed a Walkman on his ears and played a song. I totally fell apart after leaving the room."

A girl in Long Island had brain cancer and her request was to meet Steve. She was twelve years old. Steve went to see her by himself. "It was difficult. When I say difficult, I mean I've had mixed feelings about doing these kinds of things. It comes with a lot of responsibility. It took me back to where my dreams started, in the organization-because all of a sudden it's so important for someone to meet me. You have a tendency to forget what you've accomplished when you get lost in this career stuff.

"By showing up at someone's bedside, you confirm to the person in a very, very absolute way that they are terminal. That makes the commitment to show up all the more intense. Also, when you're standing by the bedside and the parents are behind you—very emotional—there is no doubt that this is happening. That is the type of intensity that this has brought to my life, and I've never taken it lightly.

"It changes your whole life. I'm never the same person I was when I got there. It confirms the limited amount of time we all have—and who knows how long that is. There is no greater honor someone can bestow upon you than to make this type of request, but it does involve incredible emotional upheaval."

7

Expectations

By the time you decide to make a substantial volunteer commitment, you will have researched the nonprofit and decided that this is an organization with which you want to be involved. You will have certain expectations of what the volunteer opportunity ought to offer and the nonprofit will have reasonable expectations of what you will bring to the opportunity.

WHAT THE NONPROFIT EXPECTS OF YOU

If you are volunteering for a one-time project, you should be prepared to show up on time, with a smile and with a great attitude.

When volunteering in an ongoing capacity, the nonprofit has a right to expect certain behavior on your part that will maximize your impact upon its programs.

1. Expect to be interviewed by representatives of the nonprofit so they can assess your ability to fulfill their volunteer needs.

2. Be prepared to attend training sessions in order to provide the best service possible.

3. Take it seriously. Always show up on time and at the right location, and be ready to do the tasks required. You should look upon this as if it were a job for which you would be compensated, even though your compensation comes in the form of "psychic income."

WHAT YOU SHOULD EXPECT FROM THE NONPROFIT

If you are prepared to give of your time and expertise, you deserve certain considerations from the organization. Bearing in mind that it is not in the for-profit sector, it nevertheless has an obligation to you to maximize your efforts on its behalf.

1. The nonprofit should provide, wherever possible, a start and an end date and a specific task to be performed, unless you are engaging in an ongoing situation.

2. The nonprofit should provide the necessary orientation and training for the task. For some activities, such as mentoring, expect to spend more than a few hours in training. For both you and your mentee, this is crucial.

3. The nonprofit should provide all of the written information necessary for you to become familiar with the tasks involved.

4. The organization should give you a reasonable expectation of the goals you are attempting to achieve.

5. The organization should be able to give you feedback and/or opportunities to assess your efforts.

Unfortunately, not all organizations are able to provide meaningful programs for volunteers. Steve Trafton is the executive director of the Henry's Fork Foundation and is candid about nonprofits. He acknowledges that nonprofits don't necessarily do a good job of providing opportunities to new volunteers, but he asks them to exercise patience and to persevere. Steve explains that for some organizations, there may not be adequate time and staff to develop programs for volunteers.

"Some nonprofits have a problem. Volunteers come and are eager to work, yet they don't stay due to program failure. In some cases they are asked to do everything at the organization and burn out quickly. Volunteers come with an initial spark, and if you don't know what to do with it, it dies out fast." Hopefully, the volunteer relationship in which you are involved provides a meaningful experience for you as well as a substantial benefit to the organization.

By the time you and the nonprofit have invested time and energy in each other, you will both have a pretty clear idea about the appropriateness of the match. If you are unsure, try to get clarity. Ask all the questions you need to until you feel comfortable.

IF AT FIRST YOU DON'T SUCCEED...

It's possible that your first volunteer experience will not be exactly what you had in mind. In fact, it may be downright discouraging. There is a good chance, however, that no one is to blame. Perhaps the organization was the correct one for you but the particular tasks did not utilize you effectively.

Bonnie Groshong is an experienced volunteer and knows that it doesn't work out every time. "The agency may not be a fit for the volunteer, not that the volunteer is not a fit for the agency." If you find the need to make a graceful exit, you should do so at the earliest possible time. Let them know that both you and the nonprofit will be better off if you separate now. Nonprofits want and deserve volunteers who feel comfortable. There are many volunteer opportunities right up your alley; the task is to find the best one for you.

THE TOP TEN THINGS THAT CAN GO WRONG

What can go wrong for a volunteer? Sometimes the problem lies with the volunteer, while at other times it rests with the nonprofit. The problem is almost always resolved by a generous dose of honesty.

1. *You have overcommitted.* This is by far the biggest source of problems. You are so eager to help that you make a commitment that is unreasonable. You spread yourself so thin that you lose effectiveness at home, on the job, and in your volunteer efforts. If this happens to you, be honest with yourself and with the organization. *Do what you can, when you can.*

2. *You missed an assignment.* Perhaps you were out of town, slept late, or just forgot to be somewhere for a volunteer assignment. If you were among a cast of thousands on a beach clean-up, the repercussions are less severe than if you stood up your mentee and breached the trust that you were attempting to build. In any case, be honest and do not commit if you are unable or unwilling to show up.

3. *The job you are doing is not what you wanted/expected.* You thought that working in the hospital would be a good fit, but you just can't get used

to the idea that there are sick people around. You love animals, but scrubbing out sea lion pools is not what you had in mind. Again, be honest. Speak with the volunteer coordinator and ask what other opportunities are available for you. If nothing fits, you should consider pursuing a different volunteer opportunity.

4. *You have been asked to be on the board of directors and find that you cannot make the meetings.* It is an honor to be asked to serve on the board of directors. In many cases, it is a way to meet influential people and is a great resume builder. However, your schedule may cause you to miss board meetings. If this is the case, you should immediately contact the board president and advise him or her of your problem. It may be prudent to decline the position at the time it is offered and consider it when attending meetings will be easier for you.

5. *You have moved to the board but would rather be back in the trenches.* Perhaps you started out as a volunteer in the organization and moved on to board service. You find that sitting around a conference table is not what you want to be doing for the organization and you would rather be exercising your passion working with clients on a personal basis. Advise the board president of your wishes and work with him or her to resolve the problem. You will be of greater value to the nonprofit if you are doing something that fulfills you.

6. *You are burnt out and need a break.* Some volunteer jobs are intense by nature. Mentoring, counseling, and comforting terminal patients can all take a lot out of you emotionally. Yet you don't want to walk away. Perhaps taking a break is the best course of action at this time. Let the organization know how much the work means to you but that you simply need a break. You'll know when to go back.

7. *You are in over your head. The training was inadequate or nonexistent.* You may be skilled and knowledgeable in your occupation yet unprepared for certain volunteer assignments. You may have been in a leadership position where dozens of employees looked to you for guidance and now you are looking across the table at a fourteen-year-old and don't have a clue. This shouldn't happen, but it does. Both you and your new friend are going to get more out of your relationship if you have the tools to make it work. If you are improperly trained, you may be tempted to walk away, and the fourteen-year-old will have been failed

by an adult once again. If you find yourself in this uncomfortable position, make the organization aware of the problem right away.

8. *The organization is not providing opportunities for peer support.* Just as training is crucial to success, in ongoing situations continuing feedback and opportunities to share thoughts with your peers are essential. Many one-on-one situations are like being on an island. Am I doing it right? What would Lisa or Fred do in this situation? Organizations that provide this type of continual feedback and training are simply more successful.

9. *The organization does not seem to be fulfilling its mission.* Every nonprofit has a mission statement, whose purpose is to set the direction for the activities of everyone involved. Sometimes an organization will redefine its mission statement depending upon successes, failures, or simply external changes. Whatever the goals of the organization, it is crucial that all involved are on the same page. If you feel that what you are being asked to do as a volunteer is not in keeping with the mission statement, you should make this known to the executive director or volunteer coordinator.

10. *The volunteer programs are in disarray.* Economic considerations are almost always paramount to the nonprofit. Survival depends on it. Therefore, it is common for the administration to put tremendous energy into fundraising and budgetary concerns at the expense of volunteer programs. Inadequate programs are worse than none at all. Dawn Lindblom is the volunteer coordinator of the Volunteers for America office in Minneapolis. "If one has a bad experience, they will tell twenty people, and if they had a good one, they will tell three or four."

A great aspect of nonprofit volunteering is that if everyone's heart is in the right place, mistakes—although they are bound to happen—will not be fatal. Nonprofits are successful when the staff, the board of directors, and the volunteers bring enthusiasm, energy and open communication to the organization. With everyone working toward the same goals, the focus can be given to the mission, and the volunteers' efforts will be rewarded.

SHOWING UP

We were not sure whether this should appear at the beginning of the book or the end, because for many, just showing up is the hardest part. Everybody with a heart wants to do something positive for someone or something else. We are biologically programmed to do so. Yet not all of us make it happen. There is a natural reluctance to put ourselves out of our comfort zone. In volunteering, this means going to a new and different location, meeting new people who may be physically different from us, performing tasks that may be challenging, and seeing people in action who are already part of a community to which we do not yet belong. Any of these reasons, and many others, can act as a barrier to involvement. Why should I pick up the phone and subject myself to failure or, worse yet, embarrassment? What if they don't like me? These are all real and normal concerns. It might be much easier at this point to think to yourself, "This book was nice to read, but volunteering is not for me," and put it in the pile for your next garage sale. Not so fast!

TWO SEEMINGLY DIFFICULT THINGS TO DO

For new volunteers, the two toughest things to do are to make the call and to show up.

Making the Call

For many, making the phone call is the biggest obstacle to volunteering. It doesn't have to be. If shyness is part of your personality, you may be apprehensive about making the call, let alone going to a volunteer site. You are not alone. The good news is that the one answering the phone is a great person. A nonprofit organization's existence depends upon its being responsive to its constituents and to the public. It does not do well raising funds or attracting volunteers if they are impolite on the phone. When we were writing this book, every single phone call that we made to a nonprofit was answered by a cheerful, helpful person. If we got a message machine on the other end, our call was returned promptly and enthusiastically. If you are volunteering, you will be treated similarly. In the unlikely event that this does not happen, you may want to think about another organization. It's not going to happen twice.

Showing Up

One way to get started is to make only a minimal commitment at first. You may not be sure about the task to be performed or the organization itself. Completing a one-time volunteer opportunity will help you to decide if you want to go back for more. You may fall in love with it or you may find yourself doubting whether it is the best match for you. It's okay if it does not work for you. Try another organization. Many people like doing one-time volunteering for a variety of non-profits and do not want to be confined to just one.

If you are able to make a long-term commitment, you still may want to get your feet wet slowly. It may be possible to observe what volunteers are doing before committing yourself. Once you know it feels right, you can make the decision to get more heavily involved.

Rosalyn Brandt volunteered to work in the office of a mentor program and knows what it feels like to be the new person. "When you go to the first meeting you feel detached. You don't know the people; you don't know the process they're going through or the issues they're dealing with. You really have to have the courage to hang in there, to develop the camaraderie with the people, to understand the issues, and to figure out how you can fit into the process," she says. While you may initially feel that you are not contributing, you might simply need to get to know the organization better. It's not because you don't have anything to contribute.

Rosalyn's experience was typical. The first day at a nonprofit is like the first day on a new job. Everyone knows everyone else, and you feel alone. Unlike many workplaces, when volunteering, both you and the staff are having more fun and feel more personally involved. It took a couple of sessions for Rosalyn to feel comfortable with the work, but the people made her feel welcome immediately.

IF YOU ARE STILL NOT SURE

You have the ability to change the world, but probably not all by yourself. It takes millions of people doing the things for which they have a passion. And everybody has to take the first step.

If after reading this book you want to contribute your time and energy but still do not know how or feel comfortable, that's understandable. However, that should not keep you from making a commitment. Even if you only have a single question, we want you to contact us. No kidding. That is why we have created the nonprofit organization Volunteer For Good whose mission is to educate, inspire and connect people with volunteering.

We want to hear from you, and there are a number of ways to contact us. Use the one most comfortable for you. You can go to the Web site www. volunteerforgood.org or e-mail us at info@volunteerforgood.org. We can be reached by phone at (800) 370-8775. Our Fax number is (415) 455-8775. If you prefer to mail us, the address is PO Box 451, Kentfield, CA 94941. Drop us a note or use the information form found on the last page of the book.

You have a lot to offer. There is a volunteer opportunity out there for you, and we want to help you to find it. Together we can.

Appendix A

Web sites Connected with Volunteer Opportunities

○ ○
Oh what a tangled web we weave…

—*Sir Walter Scott, Marmion, canto 6, stanza 17*

The Web sites listed below are national or international in scope, and may be able to connect you with an opportunity in your own backyard. They are not prioritized but may serve as a starting point for doing your searching. This listing is not exhaustive, but it provides a broad base of activities no matter what your interest.

USA Freedom Corps www.usafreedomcorps.gov
CitizenCorps www.citizencorps.gov
1600 Pennsylvania Avenue, NW
Washington, DC 20500
Phone (877) USA CORPS

On the heels of President Bush's call for increased volunteerism, the USA Freedom Corps was created as a Web-based public-private enterprise. By partnering with a group of existing organizations, the USA Freedom Corps became the largest clearinghouse for volunteer service opportunities, serving over 60,000 organizations around the country and around the world. It links with the NetworkforGood, which in turn utilizes VolunteerMatch as its volunteer search engine. As mentioned, some of the partners are private nonprofits, while some opportunities are government based, such as the Peace Corps, Americorps, and others. You can read more about them below.

America's Promise www.americaspromise.org
909 N Washington Street, Suite 400
Alexandria, VA, 22314-1556
Phone (703) 684-4500, Fax (703) 535-3900

The Alliance for Youth's mission is to mobilize people to build the character and competence of our nation's youth by fulfilling five promises:

1. Ongoing relationships with caring adults in their lives—parents, mentors, tutors, or coaches

2. Safe places with structured activities during non-school hours

3. A healthy start and future

4. Marketable skills through effective education

5. Opportunities to give back through community service

America's Promise has created a diverse and growing Alliance of nearly 500 national organizations, called Partners, which make large-scale national commitments to fulfill one or more of the Five Promises. This site connects with Communities of Promise, one of which may exist in your community.

Corporation for National and Community Service www.nationalservice.org
AmeriCorps www.americorps.org
Learn and Serve www.learnandserve.org
SeniorCorps www.seniorcorps.org
1201 New York Avenue
Washington, DC, 20525
Phone (800) 942-2677 or (202) 606-5000, TTY (800) 833-3722

AmeriCorps was created in 1993 as part of the Corporation for National and Community Service and is made up of three programs: AmeriCorps State and National, AmeriCorps VISTA, and AmeriCorps National Civilian Community Corps (NCCC).

AmeriCorps State and National
More than three-quarters of AmeriCorps' grant funding goes to governor-appointed state commissions, which in turn distribute and monitor grants to local nonprofits and agencies. The other quarter goes to national nonprofits that

operate in more than one state. The organizations receiving grants are responsible for recruiting, selecting, and supervising AmeriCorps members.

AmeriCorps VISTA

For more than thirty-five years, AmeriCorps VISTA members have been helping bring individuals and communities out of poverty. Members serve full time for a year in nonprofits, public agencies, and faith-based groups throughout the country, working to fight illiteracy, improve health services, create businesses, increase housing opportunities, and bridge the digital divide.

AmeriCorps NCCC

This is a ten-month full-time residential program for men and women between the ages of eighteen and twenty-four. AmeriCorps is open to U.S. citizens, nationals, and lawful permanent residents aged seventeen and older. Members serve full or part time over a ten- to twelve-month period. Full-time members receive an education award of $4,725 to put toward college, graduate school, or student loans. They also receive health insurance, training, and student-loan deferment. About half of the members also receive a modest annual living allowance of about $9,300, along with health insurance.

As part of the Corporation for National and Community Service, this site can connect you with a variety of agencies in your area, ranging from state education agencies to senior opportunities.

Big Brothers Big Sisters of America <u>www.bbbsa.org</u>
Philadelphia, PA, 09102
Phone (215) 567-7000

Being a Big Brother or Big Sister is something that almost anyone can do. The only requirements are a willingness to make a new friend and a desire to share some fun with a young person. Bigs and Littles expand each other's horizons by sharing everyday activities: playing sports, seeing movies, cooking, going over schoolwork, visiting museums, washing the car, taking walks, volunteering in their communities, or just hanging out together. Within those little moments of friendship lies the big magic that a Big Brother or Big Sister brings to the life of a young person—and that a Little brings to his or her Big.

BBBS professionals work carefully to match each volunteer with the right Little Brother or Little Sister and to help ensure that the relationship will be safe and rewarding for everyone involved.

Business Strengthening America www.bsanetwork.org
c/o Center for Corporate Citizenship
U.S. Chamber of Commerce
1615 H Street, NW
Washington, DC, 20062
Phone (202) 463-5517, Fax (202) 463-5308

In June 2002, a diverse group of business leaders came together to create Business Strengthening America (BSA), a multi-year self-directed peer-to-peer effort to engage thousands of America's business leaders in a campaign to encourage civic engagement and service. The business leaders have worked collaboratively to define a national, business-driven effort to engage our entire community—from *Fortune 500* corporations to small locally owned businesses—in a campaign to strengthen American society.

These companies share a core belief: an increased commitment to volunteering and civic responsibility builds a stronger society and will enable businesses to "do well by doing good" because it deepens employee, consumer, and shareholder relationships.

Citizen Corps www.citizencorps.gov
Administered by the Federal Emergency Management Agency (FEMA)
www.fema.gov
500 C Street, SW
Washington, DC 20472
Phone (202) 566-1600

The Citizen Corps supports volunteer service by promoting the safety of our communities. Through Citizen Corps Councils, leaders are brought together from law enforcement, fire, emergency medical, and other emergency management volunteer organizations. Local elected officials and the private sector help them coordinate and engage citizens in homeland security and for promoting community and family safety. The following programs offer volunteer opportunities as part of the Citizen Corps:

Citizen Corps Councils drive local citizen participation by coordinating Citizen Corps programs, developing community action plans, assessing possible threats, and identifying local resources.

The *Community Emergency Response Team (CERT)* is a training program that prepares people in neighborhoods, the workplace, and schools to take a more active role in emergency management planning, and to prepare themselves and others for disasters.

An expanded *Neighborhood Watch Program (NWP)* has incorporated terrorism prevention and education into its existing crime-prevention mission.

Volunteers in Police Service (VIPS) provides support for resource-constrained police departments by utilizing civilian volunteers in order to free up more law-enforcement professionals for frontline duty.

The *Medical Reserve Corps (MRC)* coordinates volunteer health professionals during large-scale emergencies to assist emergency-response teams, provide care to victims with less serious injuries, and remove other burdens that would inhibit the effectiveness of physicians and nurses in a major crisis.

The Citizen Corps Web site can connect you with volunteer programs in each of these areas.

Hands On Network www.handsonnetwork.org
1605 Peachtree Street, Suite 100
Atlanta, GA, 30309
Phone (404) 875-7334, Fax (404) 253-1020

Across the country, millions of concerned Americans face the challenge of finding a way to reconcile a busy lifestyle with an interest in volunteering. Local Hands On Network organizations were formed in response to this challenge, with the goal of making volunteering possible for everyone. In cities large and small, over thirty Hands On affiliates have been established in the U.S. Its primary mission is to provide support for and strengthen the existing Hands On network, while fostering the development of new Hands On organizations. See if your city is on the list and get connected.

Keys to the success of Hands On affiliates are the unique qualities it offers to the average volunteer:

- Hands On organizations develop volunteer projects in partnership with community-based agencies, then recruit and manage teams of volunteers to staff the project.

- Hands On affiliates offer strong project management, including recruitment, training, on-site project supervision, and evaluation and recognition of volunteers, acting, in effect, as the "volunteer-management department" for community-based agencies.

- Hands On affiliates offer accommodating scheduling, commitment flexibility, and team-based programs, allowing volunteers to serve with colleagues, friends, and family or to make new friends while serving with like-minded volunteers.

- Projects are conducted in a wide range of service areas to address the varied needs of each community and offer a variety of outlets for service.

- Sensitive to corporate cultures and experienced with community needs, Hands On affiliates also help civic-minded companies organize hands-on community service efforts, allowing many companies to fulfill their commitments to serve local communities while building workplace morale and camaraderie.

Idealist-Action Without Borders www.idealist.org
Action Without Borders, Inc
79 Fifth Avenue, 17th Floor
New York, NY, 10003
Phone (212) 843-3973, Fax (212) 564-3377

This is a project of Action Without Borders, a nonprofit that works to connect people, organizations, and resources to help build a world where people can live free and dignified lives. Over 29,000 nonprofit and community organizations in 153 countries are part of its network. Search this robust Web site for volunteer opportunities in your neighborhood and around the world. It allows you to connect with specific organizations through its search engine.

Learn and Serve www.learnandserve.org
1201 New York Avenue
Washington, DC, 20525
Phone (800) 942-2677 or (202) 606-5000

Learn and Serve America supports service-learning programs in schools and community organizations that help nearly one million students from kindergarten through college meet community needs while improving their academic skills and learning the habits of good citizenship. Learn and Serve grants are used to create new programs and replicate existing programs, as well as to provide training and development to staff, faculty, and volunteers.

This organization is part of the Corporation for National and Community Service. The site provides few individual opportunities, but offers links with organizations such as SeniorCorps and AmeriCorps.

Mentor www.mentoring.org
1600 Duke Street, Suite 300
Alexandria, VA, 22314
Phone (703) 224-2200

For more than a decade, MENTOR has been leading the effort to connect America's young people with caring adult mentors. Of the 17.6 million young people who need mentors, approximately 2.5 million are in formal, high-quality mentoring relationships. That means more than 15 million young people still need mentors. That unmet need constitutes what the organization calls the "mentoring gap." MENTOR works to close this gap by tackling the barriers that hinder efforts to expand mentoring.
The Mentoring.org site can link you with local mentoring opportunities.

Network for Good www.networkforgood.org

Network for Good works to advance use of the Internet as a tool for fundraising, volunteer recruitment, and management as well as civic engagement. Network for Good partners with a wide variety of organizations that deal with the multiple aspects of its mission. A number of these organizations provide volunteer opportunities, and they utilize the VolunteerMatch search capability for many of their positions. VolunteerMatch provides volunteer opportunities in six groupings, which allows you to tailor your request:

1. One-time events, such as participation in a neighborhood clean-up.

2. Ongoing programs, such as tutoring or mentoring.

3. Full-time service, such as Teach for America or programs through AmeriCorps.

4. Volunteer networks, such as Points of Light or United Way agencies.

5. International service opportunities, such as Peace Corps.

6. Virtual volunteer opportunities you can do from your home or computer.

Peace Corps www.peacecorps.gov
The Paul D. Coverdell Peace Corps Headquarters
1111 Twentieth Street, NW
Washington, DC, 20526
Phone (800) 424-8580

The Peace Corps is a government-sponsored organization that engages men and women eighteen years and older to serve internationally for two years, working in such diverse areas as business development, health, the environment, agriculture, information technology, and many more areas of interest. Currently, 7,000 Peace Corps volunteers are working in seventy countries to bring about change.

Volunteers receive intensive language and cross-cultural training in order to become part of the communities where they are placed. They speak the local language and adapt to the cultures and customs of the people with whom they work.

Volunteers work with teachers and parents to improve the quality of, and access to, education for children. They work with communities to protect the local environment and to create economic opportunities. They work on basic projects to keep families healthy and to help them grow more food. Their larger purpose, however, is to work with people in developing countries to help them take charge of their own futures.

This site is specific for potential Peace Corps volunteers and can answer your questions for this mega-commitment.

Points of Light Foundation www.pointsoflight.org
1400 I Street, NW, Suite 800
Washington, DC, 20005-2208
Phone (800) 750-7653, FAX (202) 729-8100
Volunteer Info Phone (800) VOLUNTEER, or visit the Web site at www. volunteerconnections.org.

The Points of Light Foundation, founded in 1990 by former President George Bush, is a national nonpartisan nonprofit organization that promotes volunteerism. The foundation was created in an effort to tap the creative energy of the people and its organizations in order to connect communities and individuals.

Based in Washington, D.C., the foundation advocates community service through a partnership with the Volunteer Center National Network. There are over 500 Volunteer Centers nationwide, and the foundation will connect you with the one in your area.

Senior Corps www.seniorcorps.org (see Corporation for National and Community Service)

Senior Corps places volunteers fifty-five and older in the Foster Grandparent, RSVP (Retired and Senior Volunteer Program), and Senior Companion programs. It is a national service program of the Corporation for National and Community Service, and its volunteers use their experience and skills to address local community needs. The Web site can lead you to local Senior Corps organizations.

SERVEnet www.servenet.org
See, Youth Service America www.ysa.org
1101 Fifteenth Street, Suite 200
Washington, DC, 20005
Phone (202) 296-2992, Fax (202) 296-4030

Youth Service America works with over 300 organizations committed to increasing opportunities for young Americans to serve. Founded in 1986, YSA's mission is to strengthen the effectiveness, sustainability, and scale of the youth service and service-learning fields. YSA envisions a powerful network of organizations committed to making service the common expectation and common experience of all young Americans. A strong youth service network will create healthy communities and foster citizenship, knowledge, and the personal development of young people. After entering your zip code, they will connect you with a variety of possibilities in your area.

Volunteer Solutions www.volunteersolutions.org
Volunteer Solutions/United Way of America
701 North Fairfax Street
Alexandria, VA, 22314
Phone (800) 892-2757 x320, Fax (703) 683-7822

Volunteer Solutions is a volunteer matching application, owned by United Way of America that helps volunteer centers connect individuals to volunteer opportunities in their community. It partners with organizations in thirty-nine areas around the country.

Volunteer.Gov/Gov www.volunteer.gov/gov

Volunteer.Gov/Gov is a partnership of the U.S. Department of Agriculture, U.S. Department of Defense, U.S. Department of the Interior, U.S. Department of Veterans Affairs, State of New York Division of Veterans Affairs, Corporation for National and Community Service, U.S. Army Corps of Engineers, and U.S.A. Freedom Corps. It is aimed at providing a single, easy-to-use Web portal with information about volunteer opportunities. The site allows you to search for volunteer opportunities by keyword, state, activity, partner, and/or date range.

   This volunteer portal enables you to locate public-sector volunteer positions that match your interests, skills, time, and geographic preferences. The site allows you to search and apply online for volunteer opportunities by keyword, state, activity, partner agencies, and/or availability date range. Additionally, the site provides links to other opportunities provided by nonprofit partners. The opportunities tend to be in conservation-related activities.

VolunteerMatch www.volunteermatch.org
385 Grove Street
San Francisco, CA, 94102
Phone (415) 241-6868, Fax (415) 241-6869

This online service matches prospective volunteers with service opportunities within their communities. Enter your zip code, area of interest, and distance you are willing to travel and you will be matched with a variety of opportunities. This site works with thousands of local nonprofits as well as large national organizations, such as the Red Cross, United Way, and Goodwill Industries. Volunteer-Match provides the engine for a number of the organizations under the USA Freedom Corps umbrella.

   Currently, 25,000 organizations list volunteer activities through Volunteer-Match. Just type in your zip code and opportunities in your area will appear. A great benefit of this site is that notations for kids, teens, seniors, and groups accompany the listings. For episodic volunteering, this site is terrific.

Habitat for Humanity www.habitat.org
121 Habitat Street
Americus, GA, 31709-3498
Phone (229) 924-6935, x2551 or x2552

Founded in 1976, Habitat for Humanity International is a nonprofit ecumenical Christian housing ministry dedicated to eliminating substandard housing and homelessness worldwide and to making adequate, affordable shelter a matter of conscience and action. Habitat invites people from all faiths and walks of life to work together in partnership, building houses with families in need.

Generations United www.gu.org
122 C Street, NW, Suite 820
Washington, DC, 20001
Phone (202) 638-1263, Fax (202) 638-7555

GU is a national organization focused on promoting intergenerational strategies, programs, and policies. It includes more than 185 national, state, and local organizations, representing more than 70 million Americans, and serves as an advocate for the mutual well-being of children, youth, and older adults. GU also works to educate policymakers and the public about the economic, social, and personal imperatives of intergenerational cooperation. It does not list volunteer opportunities but rather serves other nonprofits through its programs.

Volunteers In Medicine Institute www.vimi.org
162 St. Paul Street
Burlington, VT, 05401
Phone (802) 651-0112, Fax (802) 651-0599

The Volunteers in Medicine Clinics provide free medical and dental services to families and individuals who would otherwise have no access to health care. The clinics are fully staffed by retired medical professionals, currently practicing volunteers, community volunteers, and a small number of paid staff. Founded in Hilton Head, South Carolina, Volunteers In Medicine now operates clinics in many communities.

APPENDIX B

Senior Volunteer Opportunities

A wide variety of nonprofits have been discussed in this book. This appendix lists organizations with specific activities for senior volunteers. This may be a good place to start when looking for a volunteer opportunity in a field of interest to you. Other fields of interest may also be found in Appendix A.

U.S. Administration on Aging (AoA) www.aoa.gov
200 Independence Avenue
Washington, DC, 20201
Phone (202) 619-0724

The U.S. AoA is the federal focal point and advocate agency for older persons and their concerns. In this role, AoA works to heighten awareness among other federal agencies, organizations, groups, and the public about the valuable contributions that older Americans make to the nation and alerts them to the needs of vulnerable older people. Through information and referral and outreach efforts at the community level, AoA seeks to educate older people and their caregivers about the benefits and services available to help them.

Senior Medicare Patrol www.aoa.gov/smp
Phone (202) 401-4541

The Senior Medicare Patrol projects teach volunteer retired professionals, such as doctors, nurses, accountants, investigators, law-enforcement personnel, attorneys, and teachers, to help Medicare and Medicaid beneficiaries to be better healthcare consumers, and to help identify and prevent billing errors and potential fraud. Since 1997, Administration on Aging-funded projects have trained more than

48,000 volunteers and conducted more than 60,000 community education events, reaching nearly 10 million people.

Family Friends www.family-friends.org
Phone (202) 479-6675

These volunteers are men and women over fifty-five years of age who are interested in working with children who have special needs. They advocate for children who need a helping and loving hand. Family Friends volunteers are recruited from the community at large. There are no income guidelines for either volunteers or families. Volunteers receive extensive training.

Volunteers in Parks www.nps.gov

Older persons with an interest in history and the great outdoors can volunteer their time with the National Park Service's Volunteers in Parks, or VIP, program. The National Park Service is entrusted with preserving more than 360 national parks in the United States. In 1995, more than 75,000 people volunteered in almost every park in the National Park System—in big cities, in small towns, and in remote wilderness areas. Volunteers may work a few hours a week or month, seasonally, or full time. They work weekdays, weekends, during the day, or at night. Contact the National Park in which you are interested.

Eldercare www.eldercare.gov
Phone (800) 677-1116

Each year, about seven to nine million older people use Older Americans Act (OAA) services, whose delivery largely depends upon the efforts of half a million volunteers. These volunteers work through State and Territorial Units on Aging, Area Agencies on Aging, and more than 20,000 local organizations that offer opportunities and services to active older persons as well as those elderly who need help. Volunteer activities include assisting at group meals sites and delivering meals to the homebound elderly; escorting frail older persons to healthcare services, on shopping errands, and to other needed services; visiting homebound older persons and providing telephone reassurance to help ensure their well-being through regular social contacts; repairing and weatherizing the homes of low-income and frail older persons to ensure their safety and improve their mobility; counseling older persons in a variety of areas, including health promotion, nutrition, and legal and financial concerns; serving as a nursing home ombudsman to resolve resident facility disputes and to help ensure the safety and well-being of residents; providing homemaking assistance to frail older persons; and assisting in senior center, day care, and other group programs for seniors. To locate an Area Agency on Aging near you, contact the "eldercare locator" at the phone number given above.

AARP www.aarp.org
Phone (800) 424-3410

AARP is a nonprofit membership organization dedicated to addressing the needs and interests of persons fifty and older. Through information and education, advocacy and service, AARP seeks to enhance the quality of life for all by promoting independence, dignity, and purpose. It has a variety of volunteer programs available, including the following:
AARP Driver Safety Program, (888) 227-7669
AARP Grief and Loss Program, 601 E St, NW, Washington DC, 20049
AARP Tax-Aide Program, (888) 227-7669

Civic Ventures www.civicventures.org
139 Townsend Street, Suite 505
San Francisco, CA, 94107
Phone (415) 430-0141

Civic Ventures is a national nonprofit organization that works to expand the contributions of older Americans to society, and to help transform the aging American society into a source of individual and social renewal. Civic Ventures is the central office for Experience Corps www.experiencecorps.org the organization's signature program, which operates in fourteen cities throughout the country. Experience Corps places a critical mass of older adult volunteers in schools and youth-focused organizations in their communities. Started in 1995 as a pilot project in five cities, Experience Corps has grown to include more than 1,000 volunteers. Among their many roles, the older adults work one on one with young children, create before- and after-school programs, get parents more fully involved in schools, and serve as advocates for children and their needs in the larger community.

Elderhostel www.elderhostel.org
Phone (877) 426-8056

Elderhostel is a nonprofit organization that provides educational adventures all over the world to adults aged fifty-five and over. Elderhostel experiences include educational trips, university- and college-based Institutes for Learning in Retirement, and Elderhostel service programs, which engage teams of hostellers in short-term volunteer projects in the United States and around the world.

Environmental Alliance for Senior Involvement (EASI) www.easi.org
Phone (540) 788-3274

The EASI mission is to promote in senior Americans an environmental ethic that will result in the expansion of their knowledge, commitment, and active involvement in protecting and caring for our environment for present and future generations. The Senior Environment Corps is EASI's national organization that links seniors across the country to achieve sustainable communities.

National Executive Service Corps (ESC) www.nesc.org
Phone (212) 269-1234

This is an association of retired business executives who volunteer their time to consult with nonprofit and public service agencies. ESC consultants provide advisory services in a variety of areas, such as accounting, budgeting and finance, planning, marketing, public relations, personnel administration, board development and governance, organizational systems, and facilities management. There is a network of more than forty ESC organizations across the country.

National Retiree Volunteer Coalition (NRVC) www.voa.orgs
Phone (800) 899-0089

Part of Volunteers of America, the National Retiree Volunteer Coalition is a nonprofit consulting organization dedicated to creating a national movement of corporate retiree volunteer leadership and service. NRVC's unique method for mobilizing retirees to lives of community leadership and service is the Corporate Retiree Volunteer Program. Under the banner of their former employers, retirees with diverse backgrounds and interests combine their skills and experience to tackle pressing community needs, such as education, youth at risk, community revitalization, environmental concerns, and public health.

National Senior Service Corps (NSSC), part of the Corporation for National Service, listed above, has a thirty-year history of leadership in volunteer service and includes nearly half a million Americans age fifty-five and older in more than 1,200 local projects. The Senior Corps includes the Foster Grandparent and Senior Companion Programs as well as the Retired and Senior Volunteer Program (RSVP). Senior Corps programs operate in local communities throughout the United States and offer a variety of options to meet volunteer needs and interests. See Appendix A.

The Peace Corps www.peacecorps.gov
Phone (800) 424-8580

Today, almost 7 percent of Peace Corps members are over fifty years old, with more than 400 seniors currently serving overseas as volunteers. Twenty percent of all senior volunteers are serving as married couples, compared to 7 percent for volunteers under the age of fifty. Senior volunteers work in all skill sectors but are most concentrated in education and business. There are eleven regional recruiting offices around the country. See Appendix A.

The SCORE Association (Service Corps of Retired Executives) www.score.org
Phone (800) 634-0245

SCORE is dedicated to entrepreneur education and the formation, growth, and success of small business nationwide. SCORE is a resource partner with the Small Business Association (SBA). SCORE Association volunteers serve as "Counselors to America's Small Business." Working and retired executives and business owners donate their time and expertise as volunteer business counselors and provide confidential counseling and mentoring free of charge. Local chapters provide free counseling and low-cost workshops in their respective communities.

GenerationsUnited, see Appendix A
Habitat for Humanity, see Appendix A
Points of Light Foundation, see Appendix A
The Volunteers In Medicine (VIM), see Appendix A

Appendix C

Sources of Advice for Financial Giving and Volunteering

Volunteering and giving are not mutually exclusive. Whether you are interested in contributing time, money, or both, you want to know if the nonprofit is worthy of your commitment. If a nonprofit does not deserve your financial contribution, it is unlikely that it is deserving of your volunteer time. There are several extremely valuable Web sites that advise potential financial contributors that can help you assess the nonprofit as an organization for which you would like to volunteer.

While the overwhelming majority of nonprofits do great work and use their funds appropriately, a small minority do not. An article in *Worth* magazine by Reshma Memon Yaqub, titled "The Worth 100: To Give Well, Give Wisely," listed one hundred national nonprofits that she and co-researchers felt were worthy of support. A major factor in their selections was how much of revenues were spent on actual programs versus the amount spent to raise funds and administer the nonprofit. Her advice: "Industry watchdogs recommend that charities spend at least 50 percent of revenue or 65 percent of expenses on programs and no more than 35 percent on fundraising." If you are considering a major volunteer commitment to a nonprofit, you may want to find out how it is spending and raising its funds.

<u>www.give.org</u>

The Better Business Bureau Wise Giving Alliance reports on nationally soliciting charitable organizations that are the subject of donor inquiries. These reports include an evaluation of the subject charity in relation to the twenty-three provisions of the voluntary CBBB Standards for Charitable Solicitations.

The BBB Wise Giving Alliance offers guidance to donors on making informed giving decisions. It provides charity evaluations, various "tips," publications, and the quarterly *Better Business Bureau Wise Giving Guide.*

www.guidestar.org

GuideStar provides the National Database of Nonprofit Organizations, covering over 860,000 IRS-recognized nonprofits. Each organization in the database has a GuideStar report, which looks at aspects of the organization such as mission statement, goals, and results, finances, and leadership.

Over 200,000 of these organizations file an IRS form 990 or 990-EZ, while over 60,000 private foundations file IRS form 990-PF. GuideStar gathers its information from three sources:

1. The organization itself (if it is a GuideStar participant).

2. Form 990 or 990-EZ.

3. The IRS Business Master File (BMF), which contains only the most basic information, such as name and address of the nonprofit.

GuideStar does not rate the organizations in the database but posts financial information, including the revenue and expenses for the most recent fiscal year and the balance sheet. If you are considering membership on a board of directors or a long-term volunteer commitment, you may want to look at the organization's GuideStar file.

www.charitywatch.org

The American Institute for Philanthropy is a charity watchdog whose purpose is to help donors make informed decisions. Its Web site includes a section called "Tips for Giving Wisely," which provides useful information for anyone considering making a financial contribution. It also rates over 400 nonprofits on an A-through-F scale, based largely on the percentage of funds allocated for programs as opposed to fundraising and administrative costs. This can be found in its *Charity Rating Guide.*

Contact Me

I'd like to be connected with a volunteer opportunity. Here is a little information about me:

Name _____ Age _____

City_____ State_____

I would prefer to be contacted by:

☐ Phone_____
☐ The best time to call is _____
☐ E-mail _____
☐ Fax _____
☐ Mail (Enter street address)_____
  _____

Or go to www.VolunteerForGood.org and sign in online so that we can work together to find the right volunteer opportunity for you.

I would like to order more copies of *Giving from Your Heart, A Guide to Volunteering*

Fax orders: (415) 455-8775

Telephone orders: Call (800) 370-8775 toll free.

Email orders: orders@volunteerforgood.org
Postal orders: Volunteer For Good, PO Box 451, Kentfield, CA 94904

Number of Copies ____ Call or e-mail us for discounts on quantities of 10 or more.

Name _____

Address _____

City _____ State _____ Zip _____

Telephone: _____

E-mail address _____

Sales tax: please add $ 0.86 per book shipped to California addresses.
Shipping: We will normally ship via USPS Priority mail. The cost is $4.00 for one or two books and will be slightly higher on orders for three or more.

Payment: ☐ MasterCard   ☐ Visa

Card number: _____

Name on Card: _____ Exp.date: _____

93

About the Authors

Bob Rosenberg is a retired endodontist (root canal specialist). The endodontist's life is about bringing compassion to terrified patients and the delivery of highly technical clinical care to people who would invariably prefer to be someplace else. Dr. Bob is a former chair of endodontics at the UCSF School of Dentistry and has been involved in the American Association of Endodontists, having served on its board of directors and as president of its Research and Education Foundation. He is also the founder of SOFFE, the Society of Fly-Fishing Endodontists.

Bob cofounded the Ross Valley Girls Softball League, currently serves on the board of directors of the Henry's Fork Foundation, and is the volunteer coordinator of the Great Chefs of Marin benefit for the Lifehouse Agency, an organization assisting developmentally disabled adults.

Bob and his wife, Susan, have two adult daughters. His personal pursuits include fly fishing, hiking, and attempting to gain proficiency on the alto saxophone.

Guy Lampard has had a successful career in marketing in the financial sector for more than twenty years and is a partner with a money management firm in California. He is a former partner at Montgomery Securities and was senior managing director at Banc of America Securities. During his career at Montgomery and Banc of America, his roles included director of the International Department, deputy head of Institutional Sales, director of marketing, and representative on the Equity Management and Commitment committees.

Guy serves on the boards of the India IT Fund, California Historical Foundation, California Historical Society and the Heyday Institute, and is a Chairman's Council member of Conservation International. In addition to his volunteer work as a board member of numerous organizations, he has volunteered as a tutor to disadvantaged children, been the chairman of numerous fundraising events and coached Little League for five years.

Guy and his wife, Suzanne Badenhoop, live in Northern California where he enjoys golf and the outdoors.

0-595-34024-5

Printed in the United States
28053LVS00006BA/130-708